The Pieces W

The Pieces We Keep

Stories for the seasons

Katie Munnik

wild goose
publications

www.**ionabooks**.com

First published 2017

Wild Goose Publications
21 Carlton Court, Glasgow G5 9JP, UK
www.ionabooks.com
Wild Goose Publications is the publishing division of the Iona Community.
Scottish Charity No. SC003794. Limited Company Reg. No. SC096243.

ISBN 978-1-84952-566-4

The publishers gratefully acknowledge the support of the Drummond Trust,
3 Pitt Terrace, Stirling FK8 2EY in producing this book.

Cover image © Alesyafart | Dreamstime

Overseas distribution:
Australia: Willow Connection Pty Ltd, Unit 4A, 3-9 Kenneth Road,
Manly Vale, NSW 2093
New Zealand: Pleroma, Higginson Street, Otane 4170, Central Hawkes Bay
Canada: Novalis/Bayard Publishing & Distribution, 10 Lower Spadina Ave.,
Suite 400, Toronto, Ontario M5V 2Z2

Printed by Bell & Bain, Thornliebank, Glasgow

Contents

Autumn

Winter

For my dad who taught me to ask for stories
… and my mum who taught me to write them down.

Foreword

Religion generates ways of life and practical pathways. It is about being and acting all in one. When religious faith is reduced to a checklist of beliefs (tick in; cross out) then you know we are in trouble, building walls instead of bridges. Equally if religion becomes a rigid code of conduct, we are in trouble. Everyone worth their salt in the story of religion broke some rules.

That is why stories really matter. They pass on lived, remembered experience; stories are shared so we can go on living the experiences, nurturing and enriching them, in order in our turn to pass them on. You give a story, in the old traditions, to receive one back. You receive the gift of story so you can give it away again and again, without ever losing what you have received.

Katie Munnik is an excellent storyteller. She tells real stories, not the kind of artificial moral fables or concocted allegories so beloved by generations of clerical didacts. Her stories are flesh and blood, like the Christian and Jewish scriptures. They bring those big stories to life, while opening up new insights and perspectives. Through such storytelling truths are brought home to us anew – we can reimagine and rebirth the experiences, living our own lives in their light.

Through the creative telling espoused by Katie Munnik, we can join past, present and future in one carrying stream. The stories include, connect and refresh, because they are the most human way of communicating. And after all, religion is devoted to the difficult art of being human.

Donald Smith, Director,
The Scottish International Storytelling Festival

Introduction

Walking on the beach, my pockets grow heavy. My children run ahead to comb the wrack line for treasure. They look for bright pebbles and blue shells among the drying seaweed, a bit of yellow nylon rope, painted pottery, sea glass. They come to me with their hands full and their eyes shining as they show me each perfect piece. My pockets grow heavy.

At home, we need to sort through all the pieces we've found. Some are saved in jars and set up on the windowsill to catch the light. Some are meant as gifts to give – to grandparents, cousins, much-loved teachers. Some stay hidden away in pockets to be polished by fingers or held for good luck. The reassurance of small gravity as old as stone.

All this happens frequently. Whenever we walk by the sea, we come home laden with bits and pieces. There are times when carrying these treasures feels like a chore. I don't always want wet rocks in my pockets. I don't want all that weight. And then at home, the collections stack up and the house looks cluttered. Nothing is in the right place. Everything looks like it's falling apart.

Maybe that's how collections work. Sometimes, we can only see gravel or broken shards under our feet. We struggle to make sense of our fragmenting world, but we keep on piecing the world together, one bright clue at a time. We look for footsteps as we feel our way along old shorelines. We set out looking for patterns and purpose and we find maps in the stories of others who have gone before.

This book is a collection of voices that tell those stories. Some may be familiar; there are characters and tales from scripture and the history books, sitting alongside folklore and legends. Other stories spring from the world around us and speak a modern tongue. The book is divided into the seasons of the year, and reflects the liturgical patterns of the church. I have shared and performed many of these pieces in congregations and communities in the UK and Canada, as well as online. I hope that these gathered voices find their place in your own collections of useful stories.

Katie Munnik

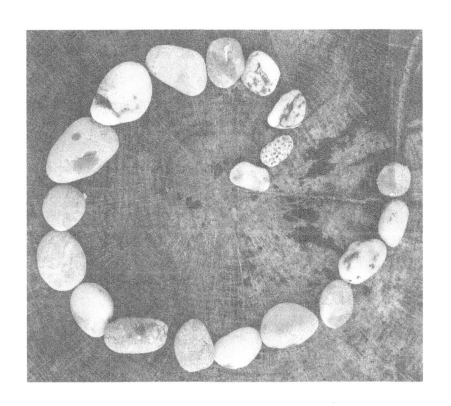

Spring

Christmas lights in March

They've been dangling for weeks. If it was up to me, I'd have been on them in January, but the boss says it is better to keep ladder jobs until the end of the winter. Might be an insurance issue, I guess, or might just be good sense. No point in slipping when you don't have to. Still, sense or no, all those forgotten strings of lights in the park are looking a mess and dangerous, too. The winds at the beginning of the month did a number on them. Snapped branches – nothing serious so we're lucky – and the trees lost balance so the loops came down. Now, it's me up a ladder and craning my neck to see where they are still holding then stretching to cut away the ties. When I've got them all loose, I'll still need to untangle them and wind them away properly if they're to be any good for next year.

They did look special in December. This year, the city requested all white lights but they didn't look boring, all the same like that. Not at all. They looked like stars. Like the stars had flown down from heaven and settled here, roosting like starlings in the trees. Fanciful, that, but that's what I was thinking when I saw them all lit up before Christmas. I brought the girls down to watch. Rosie was at work so it was just us three and that was really nice. We don't do much of that these days. They'll have homework or somewhere else to be. There was a bit of a show for the lights. City suits involved and a children's choir. There was also a van with folk giving away free hot chocolate. We stood in line, our feet cold as fish in our shoes and the pavement still wet from the afternoon's rain, but it was kind, wasn't it, to give it away like that. Just free for the asking. A bit like the lights really. Something lovely that's free for everyone. Lifts the heart a bit, it does.

Now it's March and the tulips in the park will be up soon and they are free, too, I guess. I'm paid to plant them, but they bloom for free. I wonder about that sometimes. I mean, of course I've got to eat and feed the kids. Pay the rent and save a bit because you never know, but I feel sometimes like I work and I take but I don't give back. Like I'm not quite giving enough. Rosie says guilt is a heavy habit that will only break your back, and I shrug because I'm not sure that it's guilt I'm talking about. The trees aren't guilty once I take the lights down and the gardens aren't either before the tulips come up. Just a little bare. The lights and the tulips make them better. I'm not sure what makes me better. I don't think I feel better much these days.

I used to feel it when the girls were small and I'd tell them a story at bedtime. Sit on the floor in their room and read through whatever book they wanted, anything at all. They'd pick something silly with weird names and I'd come up with silly voices then muddle through trying to keep them straight and make the girls laugh, too. They'd climb all over me then, in their zippered pyjamas. The ones with the feet, and them all knees, elbows and sharp angles at first, then they'd settle and get heavy with sleep. I'd finish the story and shift them up into their beds careful as if they were made of flowers. They always fell asleep so easy – we were lucky with the two of them. Friends said we didn't know we were living and maybe we didn't. Maybe we don't. But either way, they were angels and I'd always pray for each of them with a blessing and a kiss on the forehead just like my mum used to do. I still do it now – not the kiss because they are bigger and I wouldn't want to wake or embarrass them – but I stand in the hallway outside their bedrooms and whisper a private little blessing for each of them before I go off to sleep myself. It's a way of summing up the day. Settling it in and sealing it to keep it safe. Like a string of lights settled back into its box. Ready for next time.

St Melangell's lambs

(Psalm 46:1–3)

When I reached this place, I stopped. The silence filled me with silence.

I had crossed the waters to find a place like this and the sea had been loud with wind and birds. Sitting low in the boat, I kept my eyes fixed on the thin, wooden ribs and the tarred skin that held us above the waves. I thanked our Lord for boat-builders, sail-weavers and the strength of the men who helped me. I was even thankful for the sailors' loud songs because they pushed back fear. When we reached land and they pulled the boat up the beach, my ears felt washed and clean and my heart soothed by the hush of water washing up gently on the pebbled shore. *Hush,* I told my heart. *There will be a place.*

And now the valley. My hidden valley, a hiding place. No one would find me here or force me. No one would raise their voice against me. I could listen and pray and be at peace alone. Behind me, my mother's dreams may be filled with roses for my wedding, my father's shouts filled with curses, but here, at the foot of a gentle hill on the far side of the mountains, the air was empty, still and unfettered. My heart cried sanctuary. My crying heart.

Before I arrived, I was unsure if I should build a tower or a tunnel. What kind of cave would protect me best and keep me closed away? But finding this valley, I knew that the hills themselves were my abbey and the trees my cloister walk. This was a place to listen to the land and to the Lord.

Every running must end somewhere and my ending would be in this valley. I watched the seasons swell and swoon, the rising and setting of suns and moons to match the hatching of eggs, the fatness of apples, the falling of leaves, the quiet of winter. The Lord whispered peace and I listened.

Then one day, I heard fear come into the valley. Fear running fierce, low to the ground, a heart leaping faster than feet, faster than thought towards me. I made myself still, as still as I could manage, seated on the ground, and prayed.

The fear came close and still closer.

I spoke to my heart and opened my hands.

Then I heard the hounds. It took all the Lord's strength to keep me still. I was certain they had found me at last and I would be torn from the valley. I could hear horses now, and men's voices, shouting. Still the fear came running and I stayed still. Prayer is an anchor, a bedrock, a home.

* * *

Quick, quiver, dash, foot foot foot, hot earth, cool shadow, duck, hide. Listen. Still, still listen. Too close yet, so run, run, run. Quick feet, swift heart, fast, fast, faster yet. Be fleet, be quick, wind in the grass, brown grass running, run.

A circle, a circle, a trap but but stop now. Here? Dare? Here? Jump.

* * *

When I reached this place, I stopped. My horse found her ground and would not respond. The silence and the heat of the day closed in around me and I saw the woman seated in the clearing, my men standing around like so many tree stumps. Then that hare, a frightened brown smudge on the grass, heaving with the speed of the hunt and, as I watched, it leapt into the woman's skirts, burrowing in under her praying hands.

Were I a different man, I might have felt peace, but my heart only crashed against my ribs. The hounds circled, waiting for a signal, so I threw up my hand and the huntsman blew his horn. No sound emerged. Nothing. A strangeness filled the air and now everything was still.

A man of sound, I bellowed out my command, and the woman in the clearing did not rise.

I asked what in the devil's name she was doing, interrupting the royal hunt.

The Lord, in his mercy, gave her strength and she did not let me trouble her heart. In a calm voice, she gave me her story – flight, refuge, faith – and all the while, the hare stayed curled on her skirts. I watched as her gentle hands soothed its wild fur.

I cannot say now if it was her story or the way she told it that touched my heart. Perhaps it was the hare itself. Something in me unfolded that day and my sharp, ordered manner fell away.

I opened my hands and gave her the valley. I could do no less.

God is our refuge and strength,
a very present help in trouble.

Therefore we will not fear, though the earth should change,
though the mountains shake in the heart of the sea;
though its waters roar and foam,
though the mountains tremble with its tumult.

Psalm 46:1–3 (NRSV)

Melangell was a 7th-century saint who fled her family home in Ireland to avoid an unwanted marriage. For fifteen years, she lived as a hermit in the Welsh Valley of Llangynog, before she met the Prince of Powys, who granted her the valley and installed her as abbess. Her shrine remains at Pennant. In that area, hares are known as 'oen Melangell' – Melangell's lambs.

Walking with Mary

(Mark 3:32)

Long strides mean she is angry, but I'm not sure who is to blame. She's also scared and that one is easier. She always worries about him, especially when she hasn't seen him in a while. I can hear her muttering under her breath. *Enough is enough. He needs to come home.*

News of the scribes set her off. They came down from Jerusalem to question him and all he offered were stories. When Yaqob stopped by the house and told us this, her lips grew thin and she said nothing, only started gathering up her travelling things. The basket with thick leather straps, bread, dried fruit, and a large skin for water. She opened the old wooden chest – the one that Abba made for her when she was a bride – and pulled out a length of blue cloth to cover her hair. The cloth was rough and faded, but she held it gently between her finger and her thumb, then brought it to her face and closed her eyes. When she opened them again, she said that I would go with her. And my brothers, too. She wanted us all with her on the road.

Of course, he's been wild before. No, not wild. Just different and conspicuous. Unpredictable. He doesn't read situations well. Clever as can be, but completely blind sometimes. He just couldn't see when Abba was in a hurry, or when Immah wanted his help or his silence. He always made time for stories, even in the workshop. My favourite stories were about trees, the same trees that became the wood Abba used. Yeshua would tell us about the years of sun and rain that fattened the trunk, and what it felt like to be rooted in one place for years. He asked us to imagine the wind high in our branches and then the rain deep under our roots. That was before his travelling started.

At first, it was natural enough. We all knew that the carpenter's life wasn't for him. He said he was looking for a mentor, someone who would take him on. Immah thought that he'd find a rabbi, a prophet even. She liked the idea and it made sense. We thought that his stories might make people happy.

Maybe, we were wrong.

Now we've been walking since midday and my brothers keep pace ahead of us. I watch them talking back and forth. How do they imagine we'll convince him to come home? Our mother says little and won't catch my eye, just keeps on striding forth, wrapped up in her own fierce love. From time to time, she reaches out and touches my arm, and I know that she wants me there. I leave the worrying to her and focus on putting one foot in front of another.

My mother is a great one for walking. *Good for the bones*, she'd say, and trek us off to every festival. She loved to be among the crowds, all those people travelling together. That was the best way to do it. Safer by far and better for stories, too. My mother carried a basket full of treats and doled them out to everyone she met, sweet snacks and stories. She'd tell us about travelling to her cousin's house when she was expecting, and travelling heavy-bellied with Abba down to Bethlehem where our brother was born, then on down the Way of the Sea into Egypt, where the tallest palm trees grew and where she ate fish made red with spices.

When I was small, I longed to grow up and be able to travel far and wide as she had. I wanted to see everything, taste everything, but on our journeys to Jerusalem, my feet always got so dusty, the straps of my sandals rubbed and my throat grew dry and painful as I trotted along, trying to keep up with my brothers. So I'd stop to sort through the pebbles beside the path and Immah scolded me and told me that roads don't walk themselves. Then Yaqob and Yosep teased and made wild faces, so Immah scolded them, too, but when Yeshua smiled, she softened and said *Come on, little one. Treats ahead at the next bend in the road.* Then my big brother held out his hand and I gave him my pebbles to keep in his pocket. If I was lucky, he'd lift me to his shoulders, breaking into a gallop to catch up with our mother and the other brothers and then we'd all be walking together again until the next patch of pebbles.

I am glad that our road today isn't long. Immah couldn't keep up this pace, and neither could I. I shift the bag on my shoulder and glance up the road to the town on the hill. We will be there before the evening meal, I am sure of it. It will be good to sit and eat with Yeshua again. I hope that we can be peaceful together, that Yeshua will listen to reason, that Immah can be calm.

Beside me, she clicks her tongue and it is then that I realise she is excited. She has hidden it well. Something is beginning and she knows it. She's glad to be on her feet now and walking. She is finding strength as she goes, a strength beyond her fear and even her anger. I can't imagine what words she will use when we find him. What will she say? How can she pull him away from his travelling stories? How can any of us draw him in from the road now? It is in his blood. He is his mother's son.

A crowd was sitting around him; and they said to him: 'Your mother and your brothers and sisters are outside, asking for you.'

Mark 3:32 (NRSV)

Note: In this story, the names reflect the Aramaic that Jesus spoke.

Sacred Heart

The guy at the table next to ours has a tattoo on his chest. He's left a few buttons undone and you can see it under his shirt. I think it's a heart. So, if you think about it, he's got to be Jesus. This guy, sitting here next to me, drinking coffee just like me. Jesus. He looks a little nervous. But a lot of people do when they're sitting by themselves. Maybe he's worried someone will recognise him. Maybe he's worried he's got nothing else to do.

We like this place, me and Ruby. It's small and kinda kitschy in a good way. All basement furniture and grandma cushions. There's a dresser where they keep the milk and sugar, the spoons in old tin cans with taped-on labels. Dirty. Clean. The coffee is decent and they always have plenty of shortbread, which isn't usual around here. Ruby likes the painted plates on the wall with their gold rims and hand-painted flowers. I like the stuffed bookcases, but I don't take time to read the books because Ruby and I are always talking.

Now she's telling me rumours again. A guy on the east coast caught a lobster. Not just any lobster – this one's huge. Twenty pounds. He's got him in a tank to keep him alive, and he's auctioning him online for a thousand bucks. The animal rights people say it's a sin. But they aren't forking over the ransom money to save him. Ruby says they figure a lobster that size must be about 100 years old. I say that's a miracle. And Ruby says it's not like he can talk. He's just a lobster.

But I'm feeling uncomfortable because it feels like we're talking in parables, and Jesus is sitting right there, listening. It's like singing someone else's song right in front of them. Awkward. He just looks out the window and watches sparrows picking at crumbs. I change the topic, ask Ruby how she's been, and she says fine. She's just come home from the galleries in Washington. Ruby likes pictures and they have a lot of them there. She says she likes the way the old painters did the sky. Gold. Like it was different 600 years ago. Maybe it was. And she also says she likes the angels.

Jesus shifts his feet, drinks his coffee. Ruby keeps talking about the churches where the paintings used to hang, and about an artist named Brunelleschi, who strung churches with rigging like ships and dangled children from ropes. Children dressed as angels, and he swung them high above the congregation like holy laughter and he even had a complicated apparatus that lowered Gabriel gently down to stand beside the Virgin and tell her the good news. Spectacle, Ruby said. That's just how I like my miracles.

Jesus' shoulders slouch. He pulls on his sweatshirt, and it makes him look younger, like a kid. A 12-year-old kid, looking to skip town and leave his parents behind.

King David and the bear

(I Samuel 17:37, I Kings 1:1)

Everything happened a long time ago. Everything that mattered. These days, it's only grief and old songs. The death of sons and politics and guilt and I can't get warm and I don't want to think about these days.

So what mattered? What will I say? When it's my turn and I stand before the throne, when the Lord says all will be swept away except one thing that mattered, what would it be? A song? No. Close, but no. None of my songs are pure enough. Not even the best. So what? A woman? Michal, the wife of my youth? Or Bathsheba on that first day? Maybe. But I ruined that moment by asking for her name. So who? No one. Not even the new one – Abishag the Shunammite – who was brought to me shining, young and wearing her name and whom I couldn't even touch. I am too old and cold. I cannot love well enough any more for my love to matter.

No, it would need to be something from the beginning. The hillside, perhaps. The sky. An evening with the sheep and the doves calling in the birch trees. The clouds like curds in the west. The sun. The evening he came close. Yes. That might be it. Yes.

He came down from the mountain, unexpected as always. I spent so long watching for him, as you watch for one you love. My eyes ached and I saw nothing. No shadow, no pale shape on the grass. I must have dozed because when I did see him, he was too close. Already I could see the dark stripe running down over his shoulders, the strength along his back and the stupid sheep upwind, oblivious until he grabbed one and its legs kicked out like breaking sticks. The rest scattered. I crouched for a stone, loading my sling without taking my eyes off the bear. I stood and swung even as I found my footing and took a stand. Struck, he lost hold of the sheep and she stumbled to her feet, a red stain spreading on her white wool. Then the bear turned on me. Fear? I don't know. Death but bright death and something open without decay. A colour close to gold and another stone in my hand the perfect weight. The bear's white claws then on the grass, in the air. The Lord must have been with me between the breath and the falling. And if it had been my death, as in that moment I believed it was, I would have been content. To see such power was a gift.

Later, when the bear's breath stopped and I found courage to step close and lay my hand on the fur and feel the flesh already changing to stone, I felt something more. Absence. What had I killed? Who?

That hillside was a lonely place. There was no strength and no wind blew. No life. No word.

Yes. That happened. A long, long time ago. That moment, and, in the next, the Lord spoke into my heart. Not words but assurance. Reassurance. The Lord was still close and I would be with him. On any hill and every hill, I would be with him.

And that mattered.

'The Lord, who saved me from the paw of the lion and from the paw of the bear, will save me from the hand of this Philistine.'

1 Samuel 17:37 (NRSV)

King David was old and advanced in years; and although they covered him with clothes, he could not get warm.

1 Kings 1:1 (NRSV)

Mary's Palm Sunday

(Matthew 21:10–11)

This wasn't how I imagined it.

I had imagined this day or a day like today. A day of arrival. A procession. Acclaim. He would be welcomed and lauded with loud shouts and honour and then there would be a place for him on high. With gifts like his, a day like this must be on its way. That wasn't just mother's pride. Everyone could see that he was destined for great things.

You could hear it when he spoke. His manner is different. Right from when he was a boy, he could look right into you and speak with such directness and wisdom. He could speak to anyone. I don't know where he got that from. Not from me, most certainly. I have plenty of thoughts, that's for sure, but I carry them close. I'm not about to tackle the powers that be. That's no way to live in peace.

But this son of mine is different. He speaks out like a prophet of old. Just as I had imagined he might back when I started imagining him. Back when his beautiful mysterious life began, and then all that wondering and worrying – and now here he was. A man with a powerful voice for peace. They needed him now in the Temple, of course. That's where he should be – explaining and advising. Bringing the light that he was so good at finding in the oldest stories into these strange and shadowed days. The high priests should seek him out. They had certainly heard about him. Everyone had. So they should seek him and call him out and bring him up to a place where he might be a force for good, don't you think? Sure, he isn't from the right family and he wasn't Jerusalem-born, but he has the gifts and that should matter more. For the good of the people.

But now I worry that he is going about it the wrong way. He is spending his time trying to change the people instead of changing the ways of the nation. He is wasting his time on a very small stage. And I worry that the powers that be won't like it either. What he is doing, what he is saying about putting power – or the dream of power – in the hands of the people. It is all upside down. And all these people now in the streets are making too much noise – just like a celebration or a festival to rival the Temple festivals. What are they celebrating anyway? *The kingdom of God is near.* That's what they claim. And *Jesus, save us!* That's what they are shouting. Revolutionary words. You can't stir the people up like that and then expect a quiet life.

I wish he could have a quiet life.

Not that I expect to convince him that Nazareth would be best and that it might be time to settle down. I tried that before and he only turned away. Thought I was trying to silence him, to hide him, maybe. But, of course, it was quite the opposite. I wanted him to be seen. But seen in the right way, not in this loud, conspicuous procession. The best thing for him would be to be a wise man – a prophet even – in a small town, and then to be discovered by those who could actually do something about it. Like a promotion, as it were. Brought to the seat of power and given space and power to speak. Not force his way into Jerusalem with the rabble. Not mess around with crowds and donkeys. Of course, he is seeing it all in light of that ancient prophecy about the king's arrival on the donkey and I am sure that he believes that he is preaching peace. But I'm not sure that the Temple authorities will see it that way. The loud crowds don't feel like peaceful people. They feel like people on the edge and that's precarious.

I imagine the authorities looking down from their high places, watching. I imagine how they might see these crowds, how they might see my son and his dangerous peace. How they might mutter. But I can't imagine what might happen next nor where this crowded road might end. I don't want to imagine that far.

When he entered Jerusalem, the whole city was in turmoil, asking: 'Who is this?' The crowds were saying, 'This is the prophet Jesus from Nazareth of Galilee.'

Matthew 21:10–11 (NRSV)

Old gold

The day of the funeral, I was handed a small white envelope along with all the other papers that we'd had to sign and witness. I thought it held a coin, which struck me as odd. You don't expect change from a funeral director. Well, not that kind of change.

It sat in my pocket all day, small as a pebble and a surprising weight.

In the evening, I opened it up and found my grandmother's wedding ring. I set it down on the table so my wife could see it, too.

'I thought she'd been wearing it,' she said softly, her hand on my shoulder as she leaned in to take a look. Her fingers felt cool through the thin cloth of my shirt. 'Guess they took it off after she died.'

'They must have thought we'd want it. Because we have the girls.'

Against the pale wood of the table, the ring showed its age. Its perfect circle was softened with wear, its surface scratched but still smooth enough to catch a reflection. The band was plain with no ornamentation and no markings. No inscription inside, either, though I could just make out a series of square hallmark stamps. There had always been some haziness in the family about the dates for this generation, some questions about how long they had been married and how the Great War played into our history. The code of the hallmarks might clear the question, I thought. So the next week, I popped into a jeweller's shop where they advertised antique repair. The jeweller told me that the age and provenance of the ring could be identified quite simply, at the cost of one tenth its value. A valuation certificate would be provided that would be official for insurance purposes. I said no, thank you. I was only curious about the date. Maybe I could find a list of hallmarks online. The jeweller smiled awkwardly and told me that it looked like a very nice ring, which felt beside the point.

Maybe *very nice* usually is. My grandmother might have looked very nice, with her smart hat and sensible shoes, but those who really knew her knew she was a tough old bird, and most respected her for that. *Very nice* doesn't get you far when things get hard and there is a family to feed. That's when you need reliability and the strength to keep promises.

Leaving the jeweller's shop, I walked home beside the river. The day was cold, one of those bright spring days when the buds are fat but not yet bursting, and the sky a stretched and startling blue. I shoved my hands in my pockets for warmth and felt the weight of the ring. Sunlight broke across the surface of the river, sharp and pointed like shards of ice against dark water. I took the ring out of my pocket and it shone in my palm with an older light. Like candles, I thought, or gas lamps or torches. They say that gold doesn't tarnish. Even if you bury it for a thousand years, if you wash away the muck, the surface of the gold will still be bright.

My own face reflected there and the blue sky behind me. Just the latest reflection held by this old gold. There must have been so many other reflections behind it, layered like tree rings. My grandmother's own face, old at the end, then behind that, younger, and my grandfather's, younger, a sweetheart, a soldier, a new father, my own father as a child and the room where he was born, sunlight on another March morning. Then the war and darkened rooms and windows. A lantern in the night and searchlights in the sky, the shadows of people moving quickly. Headlines and hard news, children growing, moving away. The crush and crowds at weddings, Christmases, christenings, the noise and worry and wonder of family.

In her old age, things slowed down and grew quiet again. Circles go round. She and my grandfather moved into a home together – not a home at all. Appalling how words get divorced from their meanings. Things fall away but she kept her promises and kept beside her husband.

I slipped her ring on my finger and went home to my wife.

Jonah on the bus

(Jonah 2:5–6)

The walks were doctor's orders. Every day around the neighbourhood to keep her healthy and keep her mind active, too. She said that when you get to a certain age, you started listening to the doctors.

My mum said I had to do it. No room for negotiating. Granny's daily walks were going to be my business. I was to show up at her house every day after school and help her get ready, then tag along as she slowly walked up the street, over the block, down to the high street and then slowly, slowly home again.

It was always the same questions. How was your day? Did anything nice happen? How are your friends? Always the same. Drives you crazy like that. And then always the same stories as we passed by the same houses, the same old street corners. Like I was interested in whatever it was that happened at the corner of the high street and Allander fifty years ago. Nothing's happening there now.

I'm so done. With the slow, boring walks and done with high school, too, and the phonies hanging around there. Nail polish and touch-typing and knowing nothing is ever going to change. But I'm done. So I'm out of there. I'd be heading south if I could – that's where things are really happening – but I only have enough bus money to get into the city. I'll have to see from there. The bus is pretty empty tonight. I imagined more folk on the move. Oh well. Take it as it comes. Go with the flow. That's how to do it.

When I look down the aisle, I can see right out the front window and I'm watching the headlights shine along the road, those dotted lines getting swallowed up between the bus's wheels. I can see a bit of sky here, too, and all those stars looking down. I imagine that they are city lights, just waiting for me to arrive and then the shining will really start.

Only it's starting to rain now and the driver's still going pretty fast. We're driving through the hills and the road keeps curving back and forth. I know the ground is really rocky around here and it feels like we're underground, like we're down around the roots of the mountains, somewhere deep and hidden, somewhere dark. There's a river down in the valley below us, twisting its way over more rocks, and if the bus driver doesn't slow up on these bends, I'm worried that we're going to tumble down to find it. I'm sure it's a long way down. If I was a praying kind of person, I'd be praying now. On the last corner, I lost my balance and ended up with my head banged up against the window. For a moment, I stayed like that, catching my own eye in the reflection and I swear I looked so pale you'd think I was drowning.

The waters closed in over me;
the deep surrounded me;
weeds were wrapped around my head
at the roots of the mountains.
I went down to the land
whose bars closed upon me for ever;
yet you brought up my life from the Pit,
O Lord my God.

Jonah 2:5–6 (NRSV)

The Magdalena at the market

(Luke 23:54–56)

I'd been at the market all day Tuesday and much of Wednesday morning, too. So many things were needed for the meal. And I wanted everything to be just right. No wrong steps. Nothing forgotten. Everything put right.

There were other women, too, of course. I didn't have to do everything myself. Which was all to the good. Cooking any meal in a rented kitchen can be tricky, and this was to be a feast. I needed Martha's eye for detail, and her sister Mary's enthusiasm to keep the mood sweet. His mother, the other older Mary, was with us, too. She took on herself the task of buying bread, which kept her busy because so many hungry people came to the room to see him. Again and again, she pulled her scarf over her hair, climbed down the stairs with a basket and went out looking for a bread seller.

I counted out the feast ingredients on my fingers. Bitter herbs so we might taste slavery. Sweet spices and apples so we might remember the sweetness in work. Salt to conjure tears. Eggs for new life. Wine to bless the Lord. And, of course, the lamb.

Everything would be perfect. I was sure of that. Every dish just as it should be. And then, on Thursday evening, we would sit together in that rented room remembering the amazing Exodus story, God's love story of freedom. No. Not just remembering. It is always more than that. Each year, we hold the story like bread in our hands, and we taste it in our mouths like spices and fine wine. Freedom in every taste, every mouthful, in every home, in every year.

Yet this year was different. We were all together and that was one thing. All these people who gathered around him and with him had glimpsed this story every day. And we were in Jerusalem, too. Maybe that shouldn't matter, but I felt it was easier to find my own place in the story when the very stones around me could bear witness to the centuries of faith and celebration. Jerusalem herself helped me sing.

But it was dangerous, too. All these people. And the Romans, too. Soldiers everywhere, even near the Temple. There had been rumours of spies among them. I thought that I'd seen one in the marketplace, a tall, angled woman watching me too closely as I made my purchases, counting the eggs I put in my basket, the apples and the wine. That had been Tuesday, and I'd hurried back to the room as quickly as I could. He'd told me not to be afraid. Worry didn't help one bit and wouldn't set the table. Then he'd gone out with me on Wednesday morning when I needed to buy honeycomb and almonds. He'd walked beside me and I hadn't felt afraid.

My heart was so full on that Thursday night. Of course it was. The feast was completely perfect, but no one would remember that until much later. After the meal and the final song, the men had gone out to the garden, and in the upstairs room, there had been things to clear away and another glass of wine, another blessing shared among the women. It wasn't until hours later that the news of his arrest reached us.

Then Friday.

On Saturday, I returned to the market alone. The streets were quiet now. People stayed away. Whether they were observing the Sabbath or hiding away, I didn't know. Only a few stalls were open, Gentiles selling to Gentiles. But the spice sellers were there and that was all I needed now.

Sandalwood, myrrh and pine.

Frankincense, balsam, myrtle and spruce.

Burial spices to take to the garden on the first day of the week.

I had each one carefully wrapped for my basket and handed over too much silver. Far too much.

Walking away from the market, I held in my mind the image of foreign trees. Trees on a hillside, near a river or the sea. Orchards and groves. Gardens of trees with glossy green leaves and evergreen needles, berries and closed cones heavy with seeds. Trees rooted and growing with strong trunks to weather the centuries. I climbed the stairs to our shared, secret room, the wooden handle of my basket like a curved branch in my grip. For a moment, I paused, not yet ready to speak with the others or let go of the faraway forests. I thought I could hear the wind in their branches even then, feel the dappling light on my tired face and know a bright fragrance overhead.

It was the day of Preparation, and the sabbath was beginning. The women who had come with him from Galilee followed, and they saw the tomb and how his body was laid. Then they returned, and prepared spice and ointments.

On the sabbath they rested according to the commandment.

Luke 23:54–56

King David and the deer

Whether the time was right or the day was wrong, I just don't know. God works in mysterious ways, even in the hearts of the lazy and the proud.

To his credit, the priest did try to stop me on my way out to hunt. I was already astride my horse, my men and dogs eager to be started and the dawn creeping on, when the squat man stepped from the shadows and in front of my horse, declaring it was not the day.

I told him that he was wise, but that the sun would rise to join us soon enough.

Not the day for a hunt. It was the day of the Lord.

I laughed and said to him that if the Good Lord had meant me to spend the day in prayer, He should have sent rain. Then the men laughed, the dogs were loud and the good father turned aside with a promise to pray for me. And he did. He must have. I lived.

The day started clear though the air was cold and showed the heat of the horses. My gloves were stiff and an old scar on my hand felt thick and unworked. Such an old scar I'd almost forgotten it, the quick wound of a slipped knife when I was only a boy. My mother bound it and blessed it, telling me that I was young and the Lord was good. There should be no lasting damage. But that cold morning, I'd felt it again as I rode out from the castle and down the crest of the land, past the people in their small homes, towards the woods and the hill where the deer could be found.

We galloped past the lochs with their lingering mists and on through the trees and up to the heights to fly hawks after fat pigeons, herons and rooks. Away to the north, I could see the firth was grey and filling with haar, and Leith all but smudged away.

'But we shall have King's weather,' I said, convinced that the hunt would not be cut short. I ordered for the dogs to be released and they soon found a scent, stitching their quick way among the trees. I followed on at pace. Behind me, the huntsmen and their horses followed but mine was best and eager for the chase and my own heart beat with pleasure and something more. Vigour. Strength. Life itself. In that moment, I was the hunt, the horse, the very ground resounding and the sky above, the hawk, the heart, the life of the land. I rode hard and, though the haar now reached the trees, I thundered on.

Then a jolt and a crack and the horse crumpled beneath me. He bellowed with bone-pain as I smashed to the ground throwing myself away from his flailing feet, but the earth sloped away and I was tumbled down through rough brush. When I came to rest, I could only lie still, dazed and breathing, watching the forest fill up with fog.

The snap of dry wood away to the right. I turned for my dog but it was the haar itself, solid and white, stepping towards me. Cold fear then like a sharp knife and I reached for my hunting blade as the stag approached, bellowing. He bore down on me with certain death and, in that moment, I prayed. My mother's words in my mouth, her God the only help, the only breath. The stag paused, raised his rack of antlers with a toss and met my eye, but I was frozen. And then, as the pause lengthened, I saw what I had not seen before.

On his head, in those trees of forked bone, he wore the Christ's own mark. A shining white cross, brighter than the sun. I prayed again, this time from my own heart and not just from my fear, I swear and would swear again. I prayed that if I lived, if the stag and the Lord would let me live, I would honour Him. This place, here at the foot of the hill, would be holy ground. A seat of learning and a crown of glory to the Lord of hills and forests, the Lord of every saint and sinner. My Lord and my God.

When my men found me, they found a changed man. I told my tale and made them kneel with me in prayer, our stockings marred with churned earth, our hearts returning to rest.

On our homecoming to Edinburgh, I saw the priest still stood at his vigil so I dismounted and knelt before him, my hands gripping his holy robes. I told my tale, I did, and he blessed me. I did not deserve it, but he did and I thanked him with holy words. The good father then said he would, for the love of Christ, hold me to my glorious promise. He would see that I meant true. And by the cross, I swear that I do. From His mystery, good will out.

> Legend tells that Holyrood Abbey, at the foot of Arthur's Seat in Edinburgh, was founded after King David the First of Scotland saw a vision of Christ's cross whilst hunting in 1128.

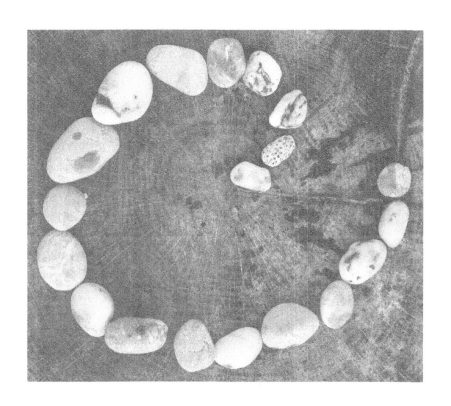

Summer

Loch Sunart – iron

There's a bit of metal on my mantel over the fireplace. It's rusty and the edges are rough, the surface marked with rings that look like old lichen. My wife isn't a fan. She thinks it makes the place look like a junk shop. Or a work-shop. Untidy, anyway, and I know it's not a thing of beauty but my dad gave it to me as a gift and I didn't know where else to put it.

Last year, the chimney sweep scooped it up with his tools and tried to take it away, and I had to chase him down the block to retrieve it. It's just scrap metal, after all. My dad is keen on family history. So he took a trip to Scot-land a few years ago, looking for names on gravestones and whatever other traces of the family he could find. He came back with this piece of metal. Shouldn't have picked it up, I'm sure, but here it is. People pick up all sorts of things. I once saw a Roman nail in a minister's study. He said an archae-ologist passed it his way. It was a great heavy thing, ugly too, and maybe that's because he told me this was the kind of nail they used for crucifixions. Or maybe it's just because old metal isn't pretty.

Dad found my piece of metal on the shores of Loch Sunart and said he believed it came from a rusted-out old boat. A floating church, would you believe it? It's a great story, this one. The boat was dreamed up as a solution to the tense political situation back in the mid-nineteenth century when the church split. The local landowner was an establishment fellow and wouldn't grant the seceding congregation land to build a new church. He even went so far as to ban them from erecting a tent, but the congregation was stalwart and met on the hillside. Over five hundred folk every Sunday outside, even in the rain, even in the snow – that must have been a real test of resolve. When dad told me this story, I said I could see where his stubbornness came from.

'Good things come from stubbornness,' he said. 'If they hadn't been stubborn, they never would have dreamed up the boat.'

Because, of course, though the land might belong to one Sir James Milles Riddell, the sea was the Lord's. At the end of their first winter, the congregation passed around a hat and gathered more than enough money to pay for the construction and delivery of their cast-iron floating church, sturdy and wide enough to seat 750 worshippers. She was delivered to the loch in July and moored 150 metres offshore and two miles down the lakeshore from the house of Sir James.

'In winter, they came seven, eight, even nine miles to gather on the loch,' my dad said, 'and in summer even more. Those were *our* people. They hiked out across the hills to get to a rebel church.' You could tell that he loved the idea – that somewhere in the crush of the faithful were folk connected to us by blood.

Maybe that's why he picked up the bit of metal. Its rusty surface leaves an iron scent on your skin when you hold it, reminding you of blood and strength. Of what lasts and what doesn't.

In the end, it was the weather that changed the story. A storm tore the floating church from its moorings and rammed it against the shore. Then even the strong will of Sir James himself could not budge it from the land. The congregation met in the beached church for years, and there must have been plenty of sermons preached about building your house on the rock, I should imagine.

The floating church has long since vanished. In the end, it was likely sold for scrap when Sir James's successor finally granted the congregation a proper building site, but bits of it do appear from time to time on the shores of the loch. The anchor still sits under the water and local people are collecting money to have it raised, maybe this summer, maybe next.

Field walker

It's a good night to walk. Some nights are for sleeping and some for company. In between, there are those when the best you can do is get yourself outside under the sky and walk through the dark. If I thought I needed to, I could use the farm and the fields as an excuse, but Jane never asks. She just looks over at me and nods as I find my cap, her hands involved as usual with her work. I nod, too. Neither of us puts a name to it and we understand each other just fine.

I don't go far. Just out through the field and up the rise, then circle home again by the stone wall where the land slopes and the brambles grow. Nettles and brambles and thistles, the borage and the lovage and the sage, as the old summer song goes. Even in the dark, I can name them all, every living thing. I've taught my kids their names, too. Meadowsweet, cranesbill and selfheal. They'll remember, whether they choose to stay here with the fields, the hills and the sheep or choose something different. What, I don't know. Some have gone to be sailors or to live in the new cities. There are new ways of earning a coin these days, but wherever mine go, they will know these names. There was a time when I thought this might be enough. Knowing the names even in the dark. It felt like a kind of prayer, a remembering that kept you rooted. I'm not sure now.

In the dark, I can hear the sheep beyond the wall, settling in for the night. I hear my own feet on the stones, my breath in my mouth and my heart in my chest. The stars are appearing now over the hill, playing that age-old game of fading just when I focus my gaze. So I shift and look away and then, quick as a bird to flight or a chased fish in the stream, there they are all over again, brighter than ever. Some things change over time, but many seem to stay the same. You can't teach the stars new tricks.

I know a few of them by name, but by no means all. Not even a handful. I guess they have them – wise folk might know or learned ones. Still, there must be heaps that have no names. Stars and other things. The weight of a promise. The difference between shadows inside and out. And then the feeling of your feet on field or sloping ground, the pull of the earth that slows you down, tries to keep you still. I don't know the names of any of these things.

I'm sure I'm not the first to think about all these things. There have been other field walkers before me. I think about them a lot, too. Other shepherds like the Bethlehem ones whose names we don't know. Then David, before he was a king, and Moses, too. He must have been a field walker. I can imagine there would have been many nights for him when there was nothing to do but walk. And he must have thought about names. I wonder what his mother named him, back before Pharaoh's daughter fished him out of the stream. Whatever it was, Miriam knew and then she stayed close over all those years, so what did she call him?

And what about God? Never did give Moses a straight answer about a name. *I am that I am. I will be who I will be.* That's something else to wrestle with.

Grey

The week of our sister's wedding, we painted the basement stairs.
Grey, not industrial, not cosy either.
Practical like nickels or skate blades,
work socks, sidewalks, pigeon grey.
We started at the top
but, after a step or two,
reconsidered.
The stairs were too steep for the two of us,
daughters still at home,
jostled for space, trying to keep our balance,
worrying about falling or dropping the brush.
So we lowered ourselves, stretched
reaching toes down past the wet paint,
elbows and knees extended as far as they would go
to start again at the bottom.

I hoped our little brother would stay where he was.
Outside hunting for ladybugs, likely,
behind the garden shed.
We should have laid newspaper at the top of the stairs
to warn him
or told our mother
or made a sign.

Instead, we decided we needed an escape route.
The basement window might work,
with a stool and a shove or two,
if we could manage to pop the bars from their brackets
the way Dad showed us, the day he installed the smoke detector.
We hatched a better plan.
We would paint every second step, then long-leg it back upstairs,
drink lemonade in the sun, catch ladybugs ourselves,
work on our perfect bridesmaids' tans
until the paint dried.

It was a good plan, twenty-one years ago Thursday.
Maybe someday, I am very sure,
we'll go back down and paint the rest.

Swimming

Light and water and sand and warmth. Peace on the way here, too, which can't be guaranteed these days. Seems of late we're getting slammed doors and tears every day, and then I stand in the kitchen, taking long, deep breaths. It's not as if I can't remember what it's like to be her age, but try convincing her of that. In such a rush to grow up. She doesn't see how soon it will all be coming her way, how few years we have left before she'll be leaving. We could almost count it out in months.

But not today.

Today, she is relaxed. Stretched out on a beach towel, her pale skin courting that perfect, golden glow and her nose already freckling. Long-limbed and lovely. She's lying on her belly, reading a paperback from the library and chewing on a pencil. From time to time, she underlines something or scribbles in the margin. I'm only watching out the corner of my eye and I wonder what she's adding to the story, but I don't ask.

We left her dad at home, working on the new cedar deck. He'll be sunburnt and spent when we get home, his skin covered in sawdust. He'll be happy.

This beach is a favourite of mine. It's not far from the city – only half an hour in the car – and we usually have the place to ourselves. My mum loved it here and used to bring us along on the bus, with a travelling rug and a thermos in the tote bag and her long hair tied back in a scarf. I'd steal her sunglasses and pull faces, pretending to be a bug, and she'd take them back and set them on top of her head, then straighten my pigtails and tell me to go collect some shells. She looked like a movie star, my mum. She'd like to be here now, I'm sure. I'd like that, too.

The sun is already hot on the sand and my skin feels tight. 'You okay here?' I ask. 'I was thinking of going in for a swim.'

'Fine, Mum.' She doesn't look up from the page and her voice is soft and distracted.

The sand is warm and dry under my feet. A breeze blows gently. Not enough to turn the pages of a book. The horizon looks hazy, and I wonder if it's the heat. Does heat do that over water? I'm wondering about this when I hear a call from the dunes, so I turn to look back and there's my daughter looking up from her book. Then I hear the crow call again. I smile, catching my mistake, and my daughter waves her hand and lets out an echoing caw. I wave back and turn again to the sea.

The water is cold, but it always is and I don't hesitate. Step after step after step until I can lower myself in and let the water catch my weight. Long strokes pushing out, the water deepens under me. Further along the coast, there are rocky stretches and cliffs, too, but this bay is gentle and so is the sea. Everything is quiet. The birds must be further out, fishing where the water is deeper or tucked away on their cliffs to watch the world. All I can hear is the sea's song, lapping and rippling around me.

I swim out a hundred strokes, counting with each breath.

A wave catches me with my eyes closed, mouth open, and I flip onto my back, full of sea. I spit out my breath and taste my heart in my mouth, wondering how a wave caught me unawares like that. I'm blinking now and everything shatters into reflected light as I find the surface again and try to balance, but another wave is coming, so I take a breath and tuck myself safely under the surface. The strength of the running water somersaults me and I can't fight it. Surfacing again, I look for the next wave, but there isn't one. The sea is flat. Relief stretches out along my limbs and then a colder thought takes hold. I look for the shore and it is gone. I turn and look and nothing. There is only white sea fog. I don't know why I didn't think of that earlier. That haziness on the horizon. Why didn't I see it for what it was? The heat must have confused me and now the fog has drifted in, obscuring everything. I do not know which way to swim. The fog is white and thick, beautiful but frightening. I try to raise myself above the water, reaching higher to see, but everything is white and shrouded. How far out have I come? There is nothing – no rocks or cliffs, no sound of birds. I could be anywhere.

I call out to my daughter, strain my ears but nothing. Nothing but the lap of water on water. My hands and feet circle to keep me afloat and I think that's for the best because I don't want to swim the wrong way and waste energy. But staying here would waste it, too. I could waste it all either way until – until there was nothing left.

I'd always imagined death would come to me slowly. Creeping and painful. I've imagined age and decline. But this was new, this idea of a sudden end. A quiet slipping away. So here I am. As easy as pushing on until I am too tired and then letting go. Letting my gripping fingers relax, myself fall away. Self? But my self feels safe, even now. My breath and my body are stretched, stitches threatened in my gut, and fear rises but somewhere tucked away inside, my self will remain, secret and contained as a child. All will be well.

But my daughter, my daughter. How long will she lie on the beach before panic flooded in? What will she do? Manage the car somehow or hike back to the road? Find help? And my husband? When would he hear? How would tomorrow unfold? I could see the abandoned tools on the deck, my daughter's crumpled clothes. My soft and private death would cut them, changing everything, even the scent of cedar.

So I choose. I know it is based on nothing but will, and still I choose. My arms grip the water, my legs kick as strong as I can and I blink against the sharp and shining light, counting my breaths, my strokes until again I feel the graze of sand on my skin, the perfect warmth of land.

I wonder if I will remember this afternoon when my time comes. The beautiful whiteness of the fog wrapping what's most fragile and the peace of letting go, a peace more beautiful for being mine.

The raven's flight

(Genesis 8:6–7)

I think about the rafters sometimes. Can't say I miss them because it stank in there. Everything was so cramped and small, and everyone got hot and bothered – all those reeking animals and the reeking folk, too. Their stink rose right up to the rafters along with all their noise. Nevertheless, there was space enough to balance there and no fear of wet feathers, even when the rain thundered on the roof overhead and the boat heaved from wave to wave. Good strong wood, gopher-wood is. And when those rafters were new, they smelled clean as the earth. I liked that. I'd like to smell them new again.

I'd like some grain, too, but there's little hope of that. Shouldn't say that – there's always hope. Just not quite yet. There's still far too much water out here. Hope must be hovering on the horizon, and that keeps receding, doesn't it? That's how horizons work.

In the meantime, I find the odd meal, and I wonder if that was part of the reason why the Man chose me. Carrion and all that. So it wouldn't be cruelty to let me go when there's hope of a meal. He's not wrong. And there are places to perch, too. Fallen trees, bits of wood. I found an empty raft a while back. Small mercies.

Can't see the boat now, so I must have gone pretty far. I'll keep flying because that's all I *can* do. There's no going back. Even if I could find my way, I have nothing to offer. No news and nothing. The Man said to bring back some-thing but all I can find is bloated and floating and he won't want that.

Wouldn't that be something, to show his wife and say – *Here, look, hope!* So I fly on. Someone else will have to bring them news.

The Man took comfort in that phrase, the one about mercies. He stood by the railing, looking out at the water, talking away to himself, listing the good things: warmth, food, family. But that last one made him weep. Made in the image of the Creator, he said, all those drowned children. As the flood grew older, he wept all the more, crying for the waste and the faces under the waves. His voice was raw and cracking like mine as he remembered all those scrambling folk who lashed rafts together with the rain already halfway up their necks. All those who sat on their roofs and screamed at heaven. But the Man only cried for them when it was far too late and even then all he could do was cry out that they were the image of God.

But aren't we all? He's my Creator, too. Why's the Man so fussed about his own face? What about mine? My beak? My shining eye? And what about my wings? All these are the Creator's gifts, too. Even the ripening fields are his and the stones and the sea. Why can't the Man see him there? This is what I think about as I fly out over these waters, waiting for the next new thing to start.

At the end of the forty days Noah opened the window of the ark that he had made and sent out the raven; and it went to and fro until the waters were dried up from the earth.

Genesis 8:6–7 (NRSV)

Junia the myrrhbearer

(Romans 16:7)

God watches the water. I am sure of that. So many gather here and everyone clutches something. A coin, a memento, a note scratched on a scrap of tin. We've all brought a token to throw away and everyone's heart aches with something. How could God be anywhere but close?

Paul will disagree but then that cousin of mine often does, so I probably won't tell him about standing here by this Roman pool. He worries about right practice and about judgement. I don't. Those weren't the things I saw in the Teacher's eyes. When He healed me and then Mary and the other women, His eyes were only full of love and welcome. There was a freedom there that I think Paul is only just beginning to sense.

There are so many things about Rome that he can't quite fathom and this pool is likely one of them. He'd say that this is a pagan place, a place of idols and sin, and he's right, but he's wrong, too. Wherever there are human hearts aching, there is God.

I'd been raised to know God in the Law and in the Prophets' poems, in all the traditions of our dusty land. Then when the Teacher spoke, it sounded too simple and maybe even blasphemous – how could God be as close as my dry, unspeaking mouth? I tried to turn away, but the Teacher's words trickled in anyway, drop by slow drop until something inside me began to wash clean and I was better for it.

This Roman pool, with its burbling source, reminds me of that. Maybe that is what draws me here. The water is lovely, flowing away over the worn rocks, always moving, always running, all the way to the sea. And today I have also brought something to throw in. It's Andronicus' fault. He bought the lamp in the first place. My brother likes clever things, and he likes the Greek potter's daughter, but I wonder at the wisdom of buying such things in these times. Andronicus brought it home and set it on our table. He filled it with oil, lit the wick, then stood back smiling as the lamp's chi-rho handle cast a clear shadow of Christ's cross on the wall. *Look,* he said, *it's Christ cast large against this Roman city.* All week, we lit it and enjoyed the flicker of light and shadow as we sat together for prayer and song. Last night, we sang the *Lucernarium*, its quiet words beautiful and strengthening:

May the Morning Star which never sets find this flame still burning:
Christ, that Morning Star, who came back from the dead,
and shed his peaceful light on all mankind.

This morning, there was talk in the market and tension in the air. The potter has disappeared and his daughter, too. Soldiers are knocking on doors. There is fear and some are going underground. We will be suspect, of course, and likely searched. Our house arrest with Paul will not be forgotten. Those who stay in our house will not be safe for long.

So, in fear, I broke the lamp. I meant only to snap off the handle, but the clay cracked and it will not hold oil any more. I hid the chi-rho in the folds of my clothes and came here to the pool. There are so many people here, mouthing prayers and tossing in all manner of things. A buckle, a marble, something like a cup. Some things splash and sink, and some land on the rocks, then sit in plain sight. A jagged broken brooch, coins like eyes. I will aim for deeper water.

I wonder what my husband would say, seeing me here like this. Junia not Joanna any more. For the sake of our good works, I have taken on Roman custom. Chuza would have loved to live in Rome. He loved ceremony and certainly had his own dignified flair. Knew how to catch the eye and shine. Perhaps that is why Herod chose him and elevated him in the household. Elevated me, too, of course, and I had to learn how to paint my eyes and dress my hair. The natural style was unacceptable and beneath our station, even as servants. Later, Paul would prod me about the red dye and the black, but I do not think that he understands the importance of custom. Had I left my hair undyed, Herod's wife would never have been receptive to my talk and she never would have heard of the Teacher. If only Herodias had worked more influence on her husband. But is that right? Perhaps not. Had my small influence managed to save the Teacher, what then? Without His sacrifice, where would His glory be? His teaching and His crown? I do not understand. I cannot unravel the patterns of what is and what might have been. Paul is better at that. So many nights he and Andronicus sat, wrestling with the Law and the Prophets, seeking and finding the Teacher's light in so many unexpected places. If Chuza were here now, he would sit with them and listen, nod, draw his cloak close and nod again, perhaps in prayer. He would enjoy their company.

There were rumours in Jerusalem that Chuza lost his job because of my conversion and my faith. Others said that he, too, began to follow the Way, perhaps was arrested, even killed. The truth was more common and far less newsworthy. Chuza was taken by the Lord without sign or miracle. Just a fever in the night, then a troubled heart and, within the week, he was gone. I washed his body and anointed him with myrrh. The same myrrh I had purchased for the Teacher and had taken that morning with Mary to the tomb.

For months, that still-sealed jar sat on the shelf, and when I opened it for Chuza, I could only weep.

We buried him in a quiet garden tomb and travelled north, Andronicus and I, trying to leave those sad days behind us. In the markets in Tyre and Sidon, we heard the rumours, then again in Myra and Salmone, but by the time we reached Rome, the rumours stopped and we felt safe. God watched the waters of our travels and we did not suffer storms. In this great city, we've learned to weather the changing moods of the powerful and find quiet ways to share the good news. Many of the Way have come to our house and we have welcomed them all. Together, we've shared what stories we know and learned from them of the wonderful new things God is doing in so many cities and villages. When Paul came to town, I was worried that his bad reputation might precede him and that the faithful might stay away from our gatherings. But I was wrong and, oh, what a table we've had here in Rome. So many came to the Way among us. We were so filled with joy.

Paul has been gone now for several months and writes that he hopes to return. It would be good to see him, of course. Despite everything. It would be good to talk with him again about the Teacher and the Way. But I won't tell him about this morning nor how it feels to stand by the pool, gripping the chi-rho cross, keeping it secret. I take a breath, a long pause like prayer, then I lift my hand and throw in my token. Mercifully, it sinks. I was right. God watches this water, too.

Greet Andronicus and Junia, my relatives who were in prison with me; they are prominent among the apostles, and they were in Christ before I was.

Romans 16:7

Junia is the Latin version of Joanna and some scholars connect Junia with the wife of Chuza, Herod's steward, as mentioned in Luke 8:2–3. In the Orthodox tradition, she is remembered as Saint Joanna the Myrrhbearer, who visited the tomb with Mary Magdalene, Mary the mother of James and the other women in Luke 24:10. Some Churches celebrate Joanna and the other myrrhbearers on August 3rd.

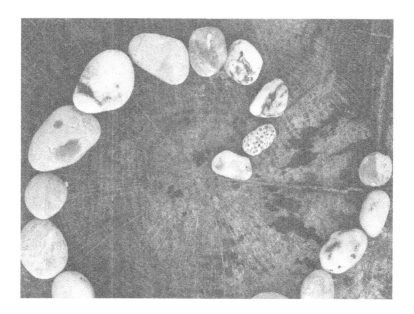

A letter to the person under the train

I didn't go to work that day last week so I wasn't on the train in the afternoon. I'd decided to work from home and the sun was so bright I had to pull the curtains to read the words on my computer screen.

When I got to the station the next morning, I saw a sign apologising for the delays in service the day before. I wonder if you thought about that. Delays. Inconvenience. All that. I wouldn't have, I don't think. You probably didn't either. You had other things on your mind.

I don't mean that to sound snarky or judgemental. I don't mean to criticise. It's just an observation. Your act – jumping under a train, not thinking about others – has made me think about you.

I don't know anything about you. I definitely don't know why you did it. I don't know how dark you must have felt. I don't even know if you are a man or a woman. I don't know if you meant to do it. Maybe you slipped. All I know I read on the formal sign at the station, and it only said 'person under a train'.

I haven't lived long in this city, but I understand this happens frequently. There are a lot of people who make themselves slip under the trains. So, you've joined a bit of a growing group. Those who see trains as weapons, the perfect weapon to turn against themselves. Or maybe their families.

I can almost see the logic in your choice. It's bound to be quick. And there is a romantic drama about trains, I suppose. I've heard also about people running down into the tunnels. One last sprint into certain nothingness, certain only that the end will come, rushing and soon. Dramatic.

But I can't get my head around the actual act of doing it. How can you throw everything away like that? Yes, seasons and trees and birds and all that, sunsets and chocolate. But what about fingers? They are wonderful, when you look at them. And thumbs. My daughter likes to play with mine, measuring hers against mine when we are talking together. We link pinkies to make promises and twiddle thumbs at each other like puppets and laugh. She likes to trace the shape of the veins along my thumb and up my wrist. She says they look like trees. She is still little. And she's learning how to read. She finds words everywhere – in newspapers, in shop windows, on signs. She knows enough words now to read a formal sign at the station. But she wasn't with me that morning, so she didn't see it. I'm not sure what I'll tell her when she does.

Just like I'm not sure what to say to you. This letter is a bit late, really. But I wanted you to know that I am thinking about you.

I can't say that I understand, but I can say that I am thinking about you.

Anna the mother

I am glad she is patient. This will take time.

With a little work, I think I can shift that look on her face into holiness.
Raise the gaze a fraction. Change her mouth. She had been perfect this
morning and I could see why the master suggested her as a model. I should
have used my time more wisely, not fussed so much with the angles of hands
and fabric. I should have memorised her face, her perfect face. But I'd been
hesitant and slow to start. Then all too soon, the cathedral bells were ringing
noon and I relented and turned away to my lunch. She darted off to the
market, returning later out of breath with a basket of new potatoes and
spring onions. It is sitting beside her now and I wonder if I might include it
in the work. Anna with the onions, perhaps.

Her hair is yellow and hangs in a heavy braid, matching the twisted handle
of her basket. I have posed her on a stool with the folds of her dress spread
out over her feet and onto the rug where her holy daughter will sit cradling
the infant. Today my Anna is alone. It's best not to crowd the place with
models. That's what the master said. Focus on what is before your eyes.

I have been meticulous with my colour planning. Anna's blue will be deep,
her hair an old gold while Mary's will be bright like morning sunlight. The
child's eyes will also shine with gold, just a few flecks, and the rooftops
behind them will be red, the river its own slate blue.

The master approved of my colour-work and assured me the composition
was strong. It is the faces that will carry the day, he said. I simply needed to

listen and let the faces speak to me.

As I ate my bread and watched the warm light on the roofs across the way, I felt certain he was right. The woman's face is perfect. Older than I am, but not yet old, she wears the beginnings of half moons beneath her eyes and soft lines beside her mouth. She is the holy mother of the Immaculate Virgin. She is Anna. Outside my window, pigeons strutted and cooed, the midday breeze ruffling their feathers, and the sun was as gold as perfect paint.

Then I heard her voice in the street below. A voice that could not be ignored – edged and raw – and I'd jumped up from my stool to look. A man stood with her in the middle of the street, a thug with a face like something dug up from the earth. He towered over her with his arm raised. I almost spoke. Of course I did, almost shouted because he couldn't strike her, it would never do. A welt would spoil everything. Even a bruise. I needed her colour, her texture, those humble, fine features so fitting for the mother of our Lady. I was just about to call out when her voice struck my ear again, clattering pigeons to flight. He dropped his hand, my own face crimson with the sting of her word. For a moment, she held him with a look, then tossed her head and, released, he stepped back and turned away.

Twenty minutes before I heard her foot on the stair. An artist's lifetime and, in that time, I did imagine that I would not see her again. That she would slip away and disappear into the city streets. I would need to begin again because how could I ever find another face like hers? I could never remember it well enough, nor invent anything as perfect. I am not skilled enough to conjure life out of simple tint. I need to look, to listen, to pay attention and then find the form. That is how the work comes. It can be no other way. I must confess, I felt despair. The pigeons resettled on the rooftop across the road and I held my breath.

And then she returned, out of breath and carrying onions. She said little, but stood a long moment in front of my glass, reworking the braid in her hair, her jaw harder now, sharper. She changed her dress and arranged the folds of cloth. I stilled my heart and sat down at my easel.

Now I watch the light changing slowly across the woman's changed face. I focus on the basket of onions. From here, I cannot smell them, which strikes me as strange. Mine is not a large room and I sit close enough to see the colour clearly. But their raw green scent is absent, tucked between their sharp and folded layers like the words we carry hidden in our mouths, strong enough to bring a tear to any eye.

Legend tells us that Anna was the mother of Mary and the grand-mother of Jesus. While she is not mentioned in the Bible, her story can be traced to the early days of the church and, in many places, she is remembered in architecture and art. Justinian built a church in her name in Constantinople in 550, and in the church of Santa Maria Antiqua in Rome, there is an 8th-century fresco commemorating her life. In the 15th century, Martin Luther left his philosophical studies and decided to become a monk after crying out in prayer to Saint Anne.

She is commemorated on July 26th and she is often depicted in art with Mary and the Christ child.

Jairus' wife

(Luke 8:41–42)

Breathless and it tastes like betrayal to speak of God. Betrayal of what? Who? I'm not sure I can say. God or the child or language itself? Because where is justice in a death like this? And as the Lord is just, where then is the Lord?

All these questions I dare not breathe.

My daughter is still and I will need to stand again, to fold the cloth, to form the words. Arrangements. Announcements. I will need to let go her hand. Not yet. Not yet.

I heard tales in the market years ago. Yes, it must have been years because I remember standing there so heavily pregnant and listening to a woman with skin as pale as bone and eyes that were blue like people from the mountains. A foreigner, though she spoke my tongue. She told me strange things from stranger lands. Months of snow. Lights that dance like veils in the sky. Geese that hatch from the sea itself. White beaches and black beaches and beaches made of glass. But people are people, she said, and everywhere women must labour for birth and must cheat death. She wanted to sell me dry leaves to brew and drink and beads to wear at my throat that would protect the child from my birth cries. I shook my head. My husband would not approve and neither would his colleagues at the synagogue. She smiled and sweet lines appeared at the corners of her mouth. She told me that in the North her people sang of swans to soothe mothers who waited and that the ancients of that land buried their lost children on the wings of swans so that their passage might be soft as feathers and swift as flight.

I think of that now and wish for something so white and wonderful for my own lost daughter.

My husband isn't here. He has gone to fetch the teacher – the one that the crowds have been following – and all because he, too, has heard tales. I have told him that the market's tales may not be worth much, but he said he had to do something. He could not stay still at her bed. So he left me here to watch alone. And now she is gone. A breath and a shudder and then there was no question. She passed from here like a lamp that flickers and then is dark, leaving me sitting in this newly shadowed place.

My love. My girl. My only little one.

I fear now that if I stay by her side, I, too, will never move again. I send word with a servant so that my husband will return from his fool's errand. Standing by the window, I fold cloth, shake it out and fold it again. It is hard to get the edges straight and I will not settle but then I won't need to because my husband will soon be home and we will do what is needed together.

But here he is; I can see him now and he has brought the teacher with him. I will send him away. What good is a teacher at a child's grave? Wise prayers will not help, and family first is best when grief arrives.

My husband comes into the room, his robe smelling of smoke, and he holds my hand with something like light in his eyes. The teacher will not turn away.

'Do not fear,' he says. I want to tell him this is simpler than fear, this loud grief braying at my heart, burrowing its stubborn way between my bones to find softer parts, the parts that weep. Do not fear.

He walks past me and stands by the bed, leans over as if to admire my lovely girl, her hair feather-soft around her face. Then he smiles.

'Sweetheart, it's time to wake up.' He holds out his hand to her and how how how but she takes it as she opens her eyes. 'Good morning, lovely. Are you hungry?'

Just then there came a man named Jairus, a leader of the synagogue. He fell at Jesus' feet and begged him to come to his house, for he had an only daughter, about twelve years old, who was dying.

Luke 8:41–42 (NRSV)

Lessons from the earth

We began, tumbled forth, kicking.
Wrapped in towels and blankets, we grew,
occupied tented forts under the kitchen table,
stole cherries, dashed
between trees and forests of legs, strangers' trousers identical
to family.

We called this home.
This cosy concealment, clambering upstairs, down
into shadows and spots of sunlight
refracted through jam jars, sunspots on the tablecloth
minnows still swimming inside.

Home.
With this night and its rain, this morning room,
this rug between our beds rumpled and your arm tossed out in sleep,
light lines both our faces,
and even now returning, the round trip like a circle,
our mother's ring.
Home.

The forever of it, you said, would linger,
and you gave me a jar filled with glass chips,
weatherworn, sea-tossed, smooth.

We'd collected that glass together, didn't we, and when?
Beach-glass, wasn't it? Yes, shards sanded and opaque
brown, green, sometimes blue but
mostly only clear.
Common bottles and jars,
now fragmented and made small, frosted like windows
already broken, already soft.

You saved these pieces for keeps
on the bookshelf, left them
behind when we left
because we had grown.

The forever of it was difficult.

The path down to that beach cut
between two banks of earth

or one, you might say, with a path cutting through.
The erosion was clear, the land crumbled away towards the sea,
and here and there, like heavy, buried buttons,
rounded rocks studded the soil,
each the size of a fist, a heart.
Around them, sediment gathered,
dry soil, years of knitted roots, fallen leaves,
and all the smaller, dusting daily gravel.

It struck me then and I am remembering now
how each of those hidden stones in the soil
was already rounded by the waves
tumbled   scoured   washed until
all roughness was
erased
and forgiven.

Moon Communion

I did not think it was the right idea. Not appropriate. Not without a minister. Communion needs to be kept special. But the minister didn't agree with me. He said that it would be a jolly long time before any minister was sent into space, and anyway, elders are ordained in the church and Buzz was an elder. When the discussion came up at session, most folk agreed it was a nice idea. I didn't sway anyone. The vote carried.

Dean, that's the minister, told me later that he wanted me to know it had been his idea in the first place, not Buzz's. They'd been chatting about the upcoming moon-landing and Buzz said that he was looking for a way to mark it, spiritually, you know. Some kind of symbol or gesture that might express the wonder of what they were able to do with God's help. Because this was beyond electronics and computers and rockets. This was something new. Dean said he could think of no better way to give thanks to God than communion.

So when the day of the lift-off came, Buzz carried a little piece of communion bread, a sip of wine and a small silver chalice stowed in his personal gear, and away it went with him right to the surface of the moon.

I watched the lunar landing with a group of people from the church. We all gathered at our house, a big mix of men and women and little kids. We dragged a couple extra sofas into our lounge but there was no way there'd be enough seating, so we made all the kids sit on cushions on the floor and we passed around boxes of Ritz crackers. My wife worried it looked cheap – she'd wanted to do a proper buffet, but I told her that no one was really coming to eat anyway. She said that was fine, it was too hot to cook, then she clipped on her pearl earrings and straightened her hair.

We all thought Buzz was going to read out some of Psalm 8 on the broadcast, but when the time came, he just invited everyone to be quiet and still for a moment and contemplate the events of the past few hours and to give thanks. Which was nice. I liked that. I'd worried that he was going to make a show of it, but it wasn't like that at all. Our lounge went really quiet, really still. A couple of kids were crunching crackers, but that didn't matter. We were all there together in the quiet, in the moment and being thankful. And way up over our heads, some 200,000 miles away, our friend Buzz was celebrating communion. It was special.

> Buzz Aldrin's congregation at Webster Presbyterian Church in Houston, Texas, has celebrated Lunar Communion every July since 1969.

Mothering

(Nehemiah 8:9)

It is evening again. My difficult time of day. When the light fades, everything slows down, and it gets harder to be peaceful even in these warm nights. I fret. I regret, let dark thoughts creep in and settle. Fear frustrates my hopes for a peaceful rest. I know that these feelings are passing; they are just shadows that will vanish when the morning comes and the mothering work begins again, but for now they are my companions in this small room and must be endured.

My daughter is sleeping, which is good because she is growing and needs her rest. She is almost as tall as me and has been so hungry lately. She holds out her bowl for a second helping, a third, and I laugh. *Again?* I ask and she grins and nods. She is beautiful and, in the daylight, that is a delight. I love to watch the flash of her smile, her teeth straight and white, the curve of her soft cheek and her long, lovely neck. It is only in the evening when she sleeps and I sit up alone that her growing beauty is one more worry, and my basket is already full. I have prayed so much and sought wisdom from the elders, but I always come home empty-hearted. There is so much work in this city; perhaps God is not troubled by the work of a single woman's heart. The High Priest is overseeing the rebuilding of the House of Yahweh, and the leaders work hard to share the holy stories of our people. They teach amidst the ruins, sharing old words in new songs. From them, I have heard the story of Hannah, which gave me such hope. Like me, she poured out her soul before the Lord and she was given an answer. A son. My request is so much smaller. I only want a voice for my daughter. But the Lord doesn't listen. Or perhaps He does, but I see no sign. I do not know. I only know that my daughter stays silent though the city is loud with building.

She has always been this way. *Mute as a stone* as the neighbours whisper. I have searched my heart for the sin that causes my daughter's grief. For so long I have been certain that it must be mine. Born without speech, how could it be her own offence? It is too late to ask her father. The dead are just as mute as my daughter. When she was born, she was quiet and the mid-wives worried that she did not shout out. But she was strong and so lovely. The other mothers in the neighbourhood used to look at me with envy and exclaim over her perfect face, her silent, cheerful ways. She grew strong and stronger and always growing. She could nurse well and took delight in milk then in bread just as any child should. When she was small I used to watch her mouth as I shaped sounds with my own, hoping she would mirror me, but she never did. Not once.

Her silence grew eerie. It is a strange thing to have never heard your daughter's voice. Not even once. I wonder if I would know it now if she were to speak.

I wonder, too, if she can hear at all. She follows instructions and works close beside me every day, listening to my prattle. Together, we knead bread, pre-pare cheese, fish and fruit, and she always knows what to do. But maybe she has watched me so well now for so long that, without effort, she under-stands what is required. In the evenings when the shadows cluster close and I can no longer see to work, I sit stilled and silent and wonder if the Lord is like this, too. Because I never hear His voice or see His mouth shaping sounds. Others may sing out what they say He says, but I am never sure. Maybe, like my daughter, the Lord is altogether different.

And I worry that all I do and all that I am might be misguided.

And Nehemiah, who was the governor, and Ezra the priest and scribe, and the Levites who taught the people said to all the people, 'This day is holy to the Lord your God; do not mourn or weep.'

Nehemiah 8:9 (NRSV)

Autumn

Wasp

There is a wasp who won't leave my office.

It's been buzzing against the inside of the window for quite a while. A good half hour or so. Sadly for the wasp (and for me, too) the window in question won't open. So I left the room, hoping that the open door and lack of witness would help the wasp to think creatively and turn the other way. It didn't work. A coffee later, nothing has changed. I hope the wasp took a break, too.

It must be hurting its wings, continually pushing against the closed window like that. It can't be happy. Which is making me nervous. If it does turn around and then notice that the wee one and I are also sitting in this small room, there might be stings.

All the waspy noise is worrying him, too. He suggests that it sounded like the wasp wanted his mummy. Gold. But he also wonders if a Lego water gun might help. Then suggests that I clap the wasp between my hands. I say that would hurt it and maybe me, but he is adamant that it wouldn't. He tells me that clapping is a happy thing to do.

I'm sure the trouble is twofold. The sky on the other side of the glass looks inviting, and the stained glass at the top of the window is bright red and green. The wasp can't turn away. Its focus is held.

I won't turn this into a metaphor. Any of it.

When I was a child, there was a swing set in the backyard. Monkey bars in the middle and swings that hung perpendicularly at each end. One afternoon, I sat on the swing, kicking my sandalled feet, and a wasp settled between the straps. I froze. I couldn't swat it away because I had to hold on to the chains of the swing. I tried to kick, very gently, to dislodge it. The wasp crawled over the strap and down along my foot. Then it crawled onto the bottom of my foot, its tiny feet and buzzing wings moving between my sandal and my skin.

Sometimes, speech is impossible, but I must have said something because my little brother ran for mum. I gripped the swing's chains tightly. The wasp explored. No wind moved the leaves above my head. Everything stopped. Except for those tiny, tickly feet.

The summer before I'd been stung at a friend's cottage. I knew how much this was going to hurt. I knew that I would have to have ice on my foot afterwards, and that would hurt, too. I thought walking would be out of the question. I might have to go to school in September on crutches. In a wheelchair even.

Patience. Urgency. Try not to breathe. Those tickly feet kept up their walk along my sole. I sat still forever. For years. And then the backdoor opened and my mum came down the steps. She, too, walked slowly, as if she was worried the wasp could sense her coming. *Hold still*, she said gently, and I watched her fingers unbuckle the strap and ease the sandal from my arched foot, making space for the wasp to escape. Dazed, it settled for a moment on the swing-set pole, then suddenly took flight, and my mother shooed it away, flapped her hands as if she, too, might fly away.

After that, I loved the swing. It became the very edge of things. The terrible perch. The place of courage. My favourite place.

Might

(Mark 12:41–42)

She held the coins in her hand all the way from home. Small coins in a closed hand. The day was warm and dry, and the way full of people. The weather must have brought them out. That would be it, she thought. Warmth and other people. Crowds draw crowds, as her father used to say. He'd said those words on her wedding day, when she had been so surprised by all the neighbours gathering in the street long before the wedding feast, clapping their hands and craning their necks. As if the whole world wanted to see her that day. All those happy faces. But today, she walked through the streets unnoticed. Old women do. The road was dusty and her hands smelled of copper.

There were crowds at the Treasury, too, but then there often were. She didn't mind. It meant more donations, more oil for lamps, more prayers offered, too, and that could only be a good thing. A few travellers sat opposite the Treasury, watching the wealthy in their processions. She nodded to them and smiled, and a young man smiled back. He had an intelligent look, like a young rabbi. Her husband had once looked like that. Kind and clever, with a young man's beard. There it was again, like a heat in her heart. She closed her eyes against the grief. It would pass in a moment. A breath or two and she could manage. God was good and close and helped her through. *Hear, O Israel: The Lord our God, the Lord is one.* Strange how it was always the thought of his beard that got her started. Always. But God was always faithful and she held to that, tightly and close like the coins in her hand. Then it was her turn and she opened her fingers to give the coins away.

The traveller sat watching, and the sound of the falling coins made him open his own fingers, his hands empty. But he held on to a wider grief. Why was this mother left with so little to give while those who had so much stood long-robed and tight-fisted? Where was the justice, the compassion, the care? She had spent her whole life giving, living open-handed, trusting that God would provide. And God did provide – enough for her to continue, enough for her to share. The other donations were larger, but wouldn't be missed by the givers. It was the old mother's coins that made the box clatter, and the traveller held on to that sound, too. If only he might catch it in his hands, hold it up to share the sound, he would make it echo out across the city, and further, too, if he could manage.

The buildings here were impressive, and he could tell from their faces that his friends were impressed. But all this would crumble. It would need to crumble. Old ways needed to fall away. When something new is to be born, everything needs to make space. He would teach them that, too, if they would listen. Perhaps the sound of the falling coins would help with that story, too. Because without open hands, nothing would change.

He sat down opposite the treasury, and watched people putting money into the treasury. Many rich people put in large sums. A poor widow came and put in two small copper coins, which are worth a penny.

Mark 12:41–42 (NRSV)

Knitting

There is comfort in following a pattern
even a difficult one,
complicated lacework or intricate
cables, twisting this way, that
making raised ropes
like my own veins now
under thin skin
like my mother's,
long gone,
gone.

Or even a modern thing, all circular needles
and knit in the round.
The designers these days
use strange abbreviations,
but with focus and time, the pattern
emerges and I only need
concentrate on one line
at a time.

God is harder.
Is that fair?
Doesn't matter because it's honest.
That's something age is teaching me.

It is best these days to tell it like it is
so I will.
God is hard.
Focus though I do, I can't always see
pattern and meaning emerging.
The longer I live, the more layers there seem to be.
And regrets. Yes, regrets.
Sometimes, I wake in the night and try to unravel
the tangled strands of right and wrong.
Love is a knotted muscle, a skein unstrung,
too many dropped stitches and you're left with a ladder.

And yet and yet and yet
he meets me.
In the light and shadow in the garden,
the heights of the oaks, their leaves falling now,
and the loud rooks at dusk
or a quiet moment in the late afternoon
in my chair by the window
with my knitting in my hands.

Chaplain

It's a fresh start, just like every autumn. New year, new students, same old goals, but a new sense of purpose. The air is crisp this morning, the light a colder shade of gold. Maybe the turning leaves change the colour or maybe it's that I know term starts this week and the summer is definitely behind us.

Tomorrow will be our first full day back. Doors open early and there will be coffee and muffins in the hall for anyone who wants to stop by. It's always a busy time for us. The students are on campus registering for courses and they need some hand-holding. Or maybe it's just the free food. Either way, we get a lot of students through the chaplaincy at the beginning of the term.

It used to be called Michaelmas term. A few years back, the university officially changed that to Autumn Semester. Inevitably, some of the faculty complained and there was even a push to get me involved. Me. As if I have any clout around here. Perhaps they wanted me to stand up for the Church, or for tradition, more likely. I stayed out of it. There are enough dragons to slay around here.

But not today. Today is about newness and beginning again. Life begins anew in this very moment. That's what my mentor used to say. Every Sunday, religious as an Anglican, though he wasn't and neither was the congregation. But he liked repetition, liked weaving words into familiar patterns so that they could slowly sink into your mind, and maybe your heart, too. I loved that. And I can still hear him. His round voice rises to my mind now in the strangest places. Halfway up an Italian hillside. In the tedium of the customs queue. Or here, in this soon-to-be-crowded hallway whilst I'm pinning up a poster. Life begins anew.

I picked up the poster over the summer in Milan with David. It's a portrait of St Ambrose, a modern sketch done in pen and ink. When I found this portrait in a small café, I knew right away I wanted it. David wasn't sure and said he didn't like the look in his eye, so I promised I would bring it into the chaplaincy instead. I'd like to have it framed or maybe mounted on a board and laminated, but for now the bulletin board in the hallway will do.

The saint is holding a beehive like you might a cat. It is a magnificent old-fashioned woven thing, dome-shaped like a dovecot. I wonder why. What is it about winged things that we like to house them in bells? I think about birdcages and the painted angels in Palermo. All these intimations of sky. One of the bees has landed on the saint's hand, its small feet suggested by just a few fine lines. The story goes that when he was only an infant, his father found him in his cradle one day with a swarm of bees on his mouth. Miraculously, the child was unharmed, and his father took it to mean that, when the child was grown, he would speak with a honeyed tongue.

He isn't a saint I knew much about, so I bought a slim book about his life in the museum gift shop back in Milan. He was the Bishop there and baptised Augustine and his mother Monica, too. I think his face looks kind. Patient, too, which must help with bees, and calm. Not joyful, but content. The kind of face I would want to wear when I am old.

I suspect many of the students think I am old already. They, of course, get younger every year. That's what the faculty say. I wonder if the time will come when the faculty grow younger, too. Maybe if I stay around long enough. When I landed here a few years ago, I thought it would be a stepping stone. Not quite sure to what – I hadn't imagined that far yet, but a temporary stop on a larger, likely more dramatic journey. But so far, nothing has enticed me to look elsewhere. There are good patterns here and perhaps I feel at home. I have been here long enough to know that questions are never asked only once and that surprises can come any day. The students all worry about the same things. Love. Money. Where to live. How to choose. I repeat myself often. I suggest listening and prayer, which are probably the same thing. Sitting quietly to try to hear what your heart really wants. Trying to find where life begins anew.

I meet with people here at the chaplaincy or out in a coffee shop. Sometimes at one of the local churches or in the park. I hurry back and forth between appointments, check my watch, my phone, my hair in the mirror. Between meetings, now I will pass by Ambrose. His eyes will calm me and give me patience. The simple lines of his bees will remind me that it doesn't need to be complicated. I think he'd like to know he's part of this work. They say he looks after students as well as bees so it all fits together.

Philip the Deacon

(Acts 8:27–28)

Turns out you can't put this work into boxes. They hired me as a waiter. One of the food logistics team. The leaders were finding it difficult to balance preaching with all the community needs, so they chose me and Stephen, along with five others. We looked after the food and the accounting while they did outreach and teaching.

But nothing stays neat, not when God is involved. It started with Stephen. Something woke inside him, and soon, he was telling stories just like Peter himself. Even started working wonders and we tried to tell him that wasn't his job but Mary smiled like she does, then laughed out loud and reminded us that you can't predict what God is going to do. She said there would always be new things afoot when it came to God. God calls and we go. We do the work we're given. We stay open and the Lord will fill the world.

Which sounds easy but it isn't. When Stephen was arrested and then killed, we all struggled. We'd known that a hard road was coming, but that didn't make it any easier. That was when I found that I, too, was given words. The Lord gives and the Lord takes away. Peter said that I was being equipped because it was time for us to part ways. No one wanted this, but Peter was wise. Some went back to their villages. Others went farther afield. I went to Samaria and fell in love with the hills. What a change you get leaving the southern weather. There's a real freshness to the air that makes me feel alive. When I first arrived, I imagined a gathering, maybe a handful of folk I could welcome and share stories with. Something humble and manageable – smaller and quieter after the enthusiasm and fear in Jerusalem. But I think

Mary would have laughed again because as soon as I started telling stories in Samaria, it seemed the whole city was on my doorstep. Crowds – and then crowds again – turned away from the temple-lined acropolis and came to hear what I had to say. I found courage – God granted me that – and the right words to reach the people. In time, Peter and John came up from Jerusalem to see and to confirm what I preached. They baptised with the Spirit and all was so very, very well.

But now I'm here on the wilderness road, confused and heading south to Gaza. And all because I heard a call. Mary was right. God isn't neat. This spot is as remote as you might imagine, but it's crowded, too. I've never spent much time on any caravan routes before, and when the angel called and I answered, I didn't imagine the dust or the speed of the chariots, the harsh words to the animals, the weariness I carry. No one wants to talk. I haven't a clue why I'm here.

A southern chariot passes me, and I hear the angel's voice again, sharp like birdsong, so I follow and run along beside. There's a man sitting there reading, his voice high and strange, his face beautiful. Ethiopian, I think, from the land of beautiful people. He looks like an important official, ornamented and respected, but it's the symbols of a royal eunuch he's wearing, so he is also unclean. I can't fathom what he was doing in Jerusalem. Who would have welcomed him there? And he's reading from Isaiah's words.

Feeling like a fool, I ask if he understands what he is reading.

'How can I, unless someone explains it to me? Can you?'

I nod. 'I think so. If the Lord will assist me.' I hope the angel speaks again because I am grasping at straws here.

The chariot stops and the official beckons to climb up and sit beside him. He holds out the scroll so that I can read the passage.

'Like a lamb that is led to the slaughter, and like a sheep that before its shearers is silent, so he did not open his mouth.'

'Is it about himself or someone else? I cannot but feel that it is about the Teacher,' he says, with strength. 'The one the people in Jerusalem are calling the Christ.'

'Yes,' I say, my heart now full. 'Yes, I believe so. The Risen Christ is appearing everywhere. Even in our very oldest words.'

'I am trying to understand,' the eunuch says, and I watch his face as he speaks. His eyes are curious and kind, and he tilts his head as he meets my eye, open to my words. 'I am trying.'

'Me, too,' I say. 'And the Lord will help us.'

Hired as a waiter, here I am again. Serving the hungry. The rich and the hungry. The powerful and the outcast. The eunuch and the fruitful and the worn and weary travellers. His word will feed us all.

So he got up and went. Now there was an Ethiopian eunuch, a court official of the Candace, the queen of Ethiopians, in charge of her entire treasury. He had come to Jerusalem to worship and was returning home; seated in his chariot, he was reading the prophet Isaiah.

Acts 8:27–28 (NRSV)

Philip the Deacon is celebrated on October 11th.

The Reverend saying yes

(John 11:25–26)

When the call came this morning, I was looking for a new bag of coffee beans. We keep the extra bags on top of the cupboard, so I was standing on a step stool, not quite balanced, with the toddler and her train set, clattering and hooting away with delight, occupying the floor below. My husband shushed her as he handed me the phone. I was supposed to be working from home today, a quiet morning of cloistered sermon writing, but everyone has my number so I didn't really expect I'd get to ten o'clock without interruption.

A body had been found in the parish. A man who lived alone, kept to himself, with no trace of family or friends. Would I take responsibility for the funeral arrangements? This voice on the other end of the line was unfamiliar, sounded young and unused to this kind of conversation. A new employee at the undertakers, I thought, and behind the necessary question, I heard a sad tension.

'Yes,' I said. 'Of course, I will.' I always want to say *yes* when I'm asked this question. I know some clergy will dodge if they can and, of course, there are times when I have to say *no*. When the parish calendar is already full and my hours already promised and over-promised. Or when the children are sick and the husband away, and all my resources are stretched. But each *no* is heavy.

'Yes,' I said again, trying to make my voice sound encouraging and confident, for the sake of the undertaker as much as anything. The toddler looked up at me from the floor and I nodded to her. She picked up one of her trains and held it to her ear like a telephone. I smiled and gave her thumbs up. 'Just send me the details and I will see to everything.' The voice sounded relieved. I passed the husband the phone, then found the coffee beans and passed those down to him as well.

'Another funeral?'

'Part of the job, love.'

'So much for getting ahead on Advent. Will there be anyone there this time?'

I shrugged and sat down at the table. The toddler said she was thirsty, so I poured her orange juice into a glass. You do these things every day, but some days you managed to see what your hands are doing. I'd used that glass as a child. It had moved into this house in a cardboard box along with the Sunday night candlesticks and the wooden napkin rings my husband brought back from Malawi. Once there was a pattern on the glass, black and red, hearts, diamonds, clubs and spades. Dad called it the mustard glass, so it must have held mustard once, back in the days when he walked home for lunch every day and my mum baked bread, made ham sandwiches, and nursed babies. My husband wonders why I like old things and I've never given him a good answer. I just do. Faded things, smoothed textures or even chipped. All sorts of bits and pieces that show the mark of time passing. He likes square white plates, brushed stainless steel, granite. I like old wood, hooked rugs, beach pebbles and sea glass.

Last year, I stood at a lonely graveside with only the undertaker and the cemetery groundsman who, as I opened up my prayer book, asked me if we might just skip it.

'There's no one here and it's going to rain, innit?'

'Is that how you want it for you?' I asked. 'When it's your turn?'

He said nothing. I started the service, my mouth filling with the wind as I spoke, my words rough in my throat.

I am the resurrection and the life.

I am.

Everyone needs to be honoured at the end. Everyone needs words spoken. Maybe it's easier to think about letting go when you know that you'll be looked after. Even in this little, spoken way. Maybe that's it.

And maybe I say *yes* to so many of these lonely funerals because I spend time thinking about my turn. And my husband's. I think about saying goodbye or not getting the chance. About how the simple patterns of our days will break and be followed by days of black, hard days of hearts and spades. I think about my kids. Please, God, let them be grown-up by then. I think about them wearing smart clothes and holding hands. And I think about the words they will hear or maybe they won't because their own kids will be clamouring or someone will cough or the wind will be loud, but they will know the words have been said and that's the important part. When flesh stops and our own words are all spent, the Word is still spoken, even in the windy city.

'I am the resurrection and the life. Those who believe in me, even though they die, will live, and everyone who lives and believes in me will never die.'

John 11:25–26 (NRSV)

The old, sad sob of the sea

There will always be
the beckoning tides, the weight of stones,
the moon held aloft
in a sky pointed with light and longing and grief,
and the old, sad sob of the sea.

But dawning, too,
because dawn will come, will always come
despite the night, the longing and the song.
The heart will sing in quiet,
every heart in every quiet,
in every window, a candle flame
pins through the cities' darkness framed,
and underneath, underneath
a Name
whispered like glory.

The gardener she thought he was

(John 20:15)

Finally, finally, the best time of the year. The pilgrims are back in the city, the etrogim are ripe and I've all finished with the tree trimming. Such a lot of growth this season, and over there by the gate, you can see my enormous large pile of s'chach. People keep stopping by, asking if they might take a few for the roof of their sukkah.

'That's what they are there for. Take as many as you like.'

I love the rustle as folk gather the trimmings up in their arms and carry them away down the road, all those loud branches cut from my garden.

I shouldn't call it my garden. I only work here. Still, most days, it's just me walking these paths and watching the weeds and flowers flourish and fade, the cyclamen and the kalaniyot. Despite the etrogim, this garden is not meant to be fruitful. It's more about beauty, a nice green and growing space for mourners to come. Most of what I plant here is meant to stay hidden. Almost thirty years now I have worked among the tombs. And twenty now since that spring.

This is a garden for the wealthy dead. Plutocrats and priests and members of the Council. That's what brought Joseph here. He wanted a beautiful new tomb for himself – a tomb newly hewn – and he paid good money for it. Then brought me along a criminal to bury. Must say I was more than a little uncertain about that. This is not a place for criminals. And then there was the matter of the guards and the Roman seal. I was worried it would give this garden a bad name, or worse, stir up trouble. Maybe it did, but not how I expected.

All through the summer that followed, women came to the garden. You probably haven't heard about this. It just happened and they kept it quiet. Word of their closed rooms leaked out and others drew close to those rumours, that growing movement, but these women here came looking for quiet, not crowds. They came at dawn, sometimes at sunset. The Magdalena, Joanna and the other women. His mother, too, with her strange, open eyes taking everything in. They didn't come with weeping. That's why they caught my attention. There was strange joy among them, strange as the sharp tart and bitter taste of the etrogim, bright as life itself. I'm not sure I understood it, though perhaps I'm growing closer now after all these years.

Most of these women have now moved away. I think of them often. I picture them in other gardens, other places of life and quiet where they can turn and face the light. His mother still comes here. She is old and wraps up well against every weather. When she sees me, she holds out her hands. I take them in mine gently and she smiles.

Later, when I am alone, I see him sometimes. I think I do. He stands beyond the cedar, there in the border country of shadows. Not hidden, just not yet lit. As if he balances on the cusp of things, and I don't disturb him. I let him be. Just like all the others who come to my garden and stand lingering and alone. Let them. It is good to find a green place. I would only give him peace. And, though I say nothing and neither does he, those moments when I see him have, for me, the feel of summer returned. An autumn day turned warm and bright, soft with the last passionflower on the vine, the sweetest fig split open, and up over the wall, the birds returning to take a backward look on all they must leave behind to seek again the sun.

Jesus said to her, 'Woman, why are you weeping? For whom are you looking?'
Supposing him to be the gardener, she said to him, 'Sir, if you have carried him
away, tell me where you have laid him, and I will take him away.'

John 20:15 (NRSV)

Sukkot is a harvest festival. During Sukkot, people build huts –
'sukkah' – which remind them of the wilderness years in Jewish history as well as the transience and fragility of our lives. 'S'chach' is the
leafy material used to cover the sukkah and etrogim are yellow-
skinned citrus fruits enjoyed during Sukkot.

Everyone will be welcomed

I am not a religious person.

I'm not even one of those people who grew up going to Sunday school. I was raised secular. Even taught to write that on forms. But we went to church at Christmas with my grandparents. Easter sometimes, too. My mum said it was important. A family thing. So, secular – apart from family things.

I'm not sure what I believe. There might be something. Something must have started everything and maybe there'll be something after we die. I don't know. Something maybe. This might be what I want, rather than what I believe. Is that something different? I don't really think about it a lot. Most of the time, it doesn't seem to matter, one way or the other.

Regardless of all that, I like to spend time in the church down the street. Not on Sundays – far too many people about then and it would feel rude to sit with them when I'm only interested in the place, not in whatever it is they do.

Luckily, the church is open during the week. They hang a sign out front: THE CHURCH IS OPEN! The exclamation mark kills me. It makes you think something exuberant might be happening inside but whenever I go, it isn't. Just a couple of old women sitting at the back, keeping an eye on things. They say hello to me and let me pass. Sometimes, I see other people, too, sitting here and there, praying maybe. The first time, I guess I'd expected candles because I was surprised when I didn't see them. Not sure where I got that idea. There weren't any candles at my grandparents' church.

A bit of a movie idea. The hero seeks refuge in a church at the point of crisis. Lights a candle. Symbolism connects. All is well again, somehow. Goes home again to his wife and kids renewed for whatever happens next. God bless Jimmy Stewart or whoever it was. And God bless me.

There's not much to look at, though the stained-glass windows are nice. Simple and restrained. Sometimes, I walk up one side to look at the plaques on the wall, walking slowly, thinking museum thoughts. Memorials to ministers and their devoted wives. One beloved. And a large one honouring those who had given the supreme sacrifice in the First and Second World Wars. I find the term jarring. *World War*. Banal now, but when it was first uttered? What a concept. I wondered who had first penned that phrase. Didn't leave anyone out, did they? Jungle tribes in the Amazon, Inuit in the Arctic. I guess they were Eskimos then, right? What was 1916 like there? I've read that most folk up north didn't use last names until the 1970s. A different world.

These days, I tend just to sit. I like watching the light come in through the windows. It's a quiet place. It's good.

Highway 7

Another test and this time, she wants me there. When she mentioned *a procedure* on the telephone, I thought she was trying to spare me the details. Later, I realised that the word just slipped her mind. It isn't usually her memory that proves the problem. Sharp as a tack, my Mum, now and always, but she is getting old and I suppose words flutter off.

I know the highway well. Most weeks, I'm driving back and forth to see her for tests or company and a cup of tea. Two hours of worry on the way there, two hours of worry again on the way home. The last couple weeks, the leaves have been wonderful along this highway. It's been a good year for colour. Then over this past weekend, we had a doozy of a storm and the wind got most of them down. It's easier now to see the shape of the land, but not as picturesque by far.

This used to be our weekend drive when I was growing up. It was just two hours to the lake to visit granny, the backseat a jumble of kids and shoes, magazines, crayons and apples in case we got thirsty on the way. We'd play I spy or count the scarecrows, my brothers cheating like mad until I gave up and took to daydreaming with my nose against the window. I kept my eye open for the places where the road cut through the hills, where the drill marks for the dynamite were visible on the grey limestone layers. Dad called these cliffs 'the Rockies' and I believed they were mountains.

In the summer, we'd stop halfway for ice cream at a convenience store with deep cardboard tubs in the freezer – vanilla, chocolate, strawberry. My brothers always wanted chocolate and thought Dad's choice of vanilla was as boring as water.

Not far from the store, an old railway line cut close to the road, past a sunken stretch of swampy brush and sometimes we took a walk out there to stretch our legs and look for eagles. Dad would dig out the binoculars from under the front seat and Mum put on her sunhat – glamour with a navy blue ribbon like a movie star. Eagles build their eyries like ramshackle rafts high in the branches of drowned trees. Sometimes, there were chicks and we could watch the adults ferrying back and forth with scraps of food. I remember once we stopped on a windy day and, even from the car, we could see the little, ruffle-feathered chicks perched on the edge of their nest, stretching their wings. Dad lifted us to stand up on the bumper and we had to hold hands to keep our balance. Then a gust of wind swept Mum's hat right off her head and Dad caught it without thinking. Simply reached up and plucked it from the air like he was picking an apple. He put it on his own head and pulled a face to make us giggle and Mum didn't notice a thing. She just kept watching those little chicks with her eyes absolutely glued to the binoculars, her smile wingspan wide.

Today, the road is quiet and I wonder about stopping at the eagles. Of course, it's too cold for ice cream but I could do with a break from driving and, at this time of year, they'll be focused on nest repair. Dad used to say that if they work hard when the leaves come down, it makes the spring a little easier when it finally arrives.

Mum moved back to the lake a few years ago. Said that she wanted a new start but we all knew that after Dad died, she just wanted to go home. She bought a little house and joined the local church choir. She's made plenty of friends and even met up with some of her oldest ones, too. Tells everyone that the local hospital is a good one and that the winters aren't so hard by the lake. The moderating effect of water, she says. Everything seems to be working out fine and there's nothing to be scared of.

I think she means that. She's trying to be open for whatever comes. When I visit, I often find her Bible on the table beside her bed. It's well worn and littered with bookmarks. Sometimes, she'll tell me about something she's read or has been thinking about. Like all the advice in the Bible, she says it boils down to two ideas.

'Don't be afraid – that's the first one,' she said. 'Just like the angels say at Christmas. That's what they tell everyone. Do not be afraid.'

'And the other one?' I asked.

'Remember.' She smiled as she told me this and held out her hand to give mine a squeeze. Then she told me that the second one is easier by far, but isn't that always the way with advice?

She's remembering Dad a lot these days. Maybe it's the hospital triggering that, but so many things are bubbling up. All the little moments. The look on his face when he passed her the sugar for her coffee. Or the noise he made when he spotted something ridiculous in the morning paper.

When I get to the hospital, I'll remind her about the eagles. And about Dad in her sunhat and she'll laugh. If she has the energy today, she'll laugh. The nurses tell me that I need to be ready. Not yet, they say, but soon. I think they might be wrong, but then again, they might be right. I don't know what to think. Last week, I found the minister from the church there at her bedside and I could have cried to see him. I know he's not the kind for last rites and deathbed confessions, but there is something final about praying at a bedside like that.

I wondered if he was praying for healing and if that's what she'd want now anyway. Would she want everything fixed like that? What would fixed even mean? She won't be driving any more and her eyes aren't strong enough for birdwatching. So would she be thankful? Or is she just ready to fly away?

Sarah, now

(Genesis 18:10–11)

Our friends are leaving now, coats and children gathered, hands clasped and held, and faces kissed one last time. Dry oak leaves rustle over our heads as we trade goodbyes. I'm sure the weather is turning. The sun hangs winter-low, rosehip red. That was my mother's image. I remember her repeating this to herself every winter, tasting the old bittersweet words again.

We spent the afternoon in bright sunshine. The children chased dogs and each other, collected grasses and we taught them how to twist them into crowns. Adah, with her black eyes bright, showed them that chewing the ends makes them soft and easier to splice and also makes your spit green. Isaac loved that. His shy eyes looked barely able to believe that I'd let him try but, in no time at all, there he was, spitting with the best of them. Adah's boys are wild and fun, laughing like their mother, but you can tell that when they are grown, they'll have their father's strength. Broad-shouldered, kind and responsible. He and Abraham walked on ahead like brothers, each making plans for the winter ahead.

Soon, we'll be baking loaves of hard bread for our journeys and again fixing straps to our baskets of grain and jugs of oil. There will be wineskins and water skins and spears for the men. I, too, will wear a blade, hidden away beneath my shawls. Some of the women won't carry them, worried that any weapon might be snatched and used against them, but I've always preferred to arm myself with more than protest. Roads can be hard places for any of us.

If it were up to me, we'd all stay the winter here. It's good land and Adah and Mahol are good friends to us. It's been so long since we've been settled anywhere and been able to have friends. But the men have other plans. They say it is time to decamp, to find better pastures for the season ahead.

Tonight in the tent, I will light two lamps. The first is my mother's old lamp, made of rich, red clay and reminding me of home. The second is a newer friend, made of carved black stone, given to me by Adah when Isaac was weaned. I will light the second flame from the first, and together they will keep the shadows at bay when our night grows still and colder.

I do not know how we will grow old, my Abraham and I. It seems we already did. Long ago and back before this journeying began. Before our hard days and dangerous nights. Before the kings and the lies, Pharaoh and that rot Abraham said about me being his sister. And before the promises, too. Long before our son. In our settled days, I believed I'd grown old and luckless with empty arms as all the other wives around grew fat and happy. My dry lips cracked and would not smile, the soles of my feet ached and I did not leave the tent. I lay in bed. I could not bear to visit the well. When my time came each month, I wept and would not accept wine. Then Abraham, my Abraham, would smooth his hand along the length of my spine, caressing the knots of my bones, and the hollows of my joints. He rubbed olive oil into my skin, traced the curve of my cheek, my chin, my neck, and whispered love, love, only love. He was a faithful man.

In time, we learned to wait. To sit together in the heat of the day and find it was enough to be together. To watch the moon and not expect fullness. We even learned to shrug and speak lightly. The wisdom that comes with age. And we were sufficient. I stopped searching my Abraham's face for a glimpse of our unborn children and only watched the stars.

Then, out of the blue, Abraham heard something. *Leave and let go. Leave your country, your family and your father's house.* I wondered then, and I still wonder now, why Abraham did not take God at his word. Because, though he did leave, he didn't leave me, did he? Nor Lot? Just who did he think his family might be if not the two of us? And he took all we had – tents and supplies for the journey, animals and servants, too. We crowded the road with our leaving, the whole kit and caboodle and Abraham at the head. I say that as if he had to drag me along, but of course, I was glad to go. I needed a new start, too. The road wasn't easy and we had our share of troubles and mistakes. But what would I do without Abraham? And who would I be?

And now? Who are we now? Parents. Immigrants. Strangers. Maybe one day we'll have land of our own again, a small plot bought, four hundred shekels traded for a place of our own. In the meantime, we come and go.

This isn't the first time we've stopped at the oak and I suspect we will return again. Adah and I have made plans for more summer meals, more afternoons in the sunlight. This is land where the herds grow fat and where we can rest and be together. Standing here now in the dusk, watching our friends' shadows move along the road, I feel the old oak roots growing underneath us. They push deep, a wide, hiding circle as broad as the branches over our heads, holding on to this earth much as we are.

Our son is sleeping now. He fell asleep with the younger ones, the serving women's children, who sleep together like puppies in a pile. I disentangled him and wrapped him in a blanket, carrying him in my arms to his own corner where he might be most peaceful. His sleeping face looked young, younger than his summers, and ruddy like my own brother's face, my lovely little lamb.

… And Sarah was listening at the tent entrance behind him. Now Abraham and Sarah were old, advanced in age …

Genesis 18:10–11 (NRSV)

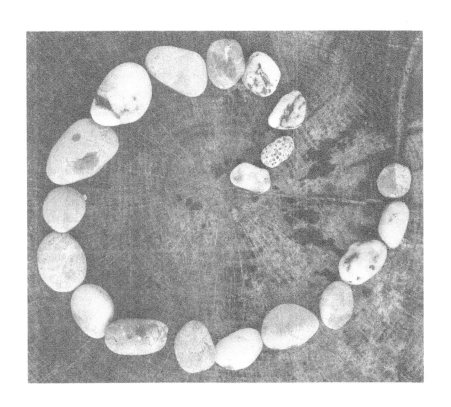

Winter

Isaiah, listening

(Isaiah 9:1–6)

The room is dark; the street below the window quiet. Pulled from sleep like a stubborn tooth, I now lie still, listening. My wife is sleeping and the children, too. So, what woke me? The students, perhaps. But their room is beyond the courtyard and they are a quiet lot anyway. Maybe there had been a cart in the street. A man setting out early on his way to the market. Or a woman fetching water in the night. Or maybe just a cat. The window is still black and dawn feels a long way off, but there is nothing to be done. Awake is awake and all I can do now is listen.

Listening is my work and it happens everywhere, at every time of day. The Voice is never far away no matter how hidden the Face might be. Sometimes, the Voice is loud, vibrant, clear and ringing and I shake as I sing out Its anger. *Woe!* and *No One!* and softer now *On That Day.* There are also times when I need to strain to hear and I have wondered if it gets harder with each king I serve. Ahaz is my third and these listening days are difficult indeed. We sit together and he offers me grapes, split figs, ripe cheese. He sits with a flaccid, pious face and says he is all ears. I do not know who he means to fool with this performance. If it were me, surely that would mean that he cared about my thoughts. That he listened to me. But he doesn't. He won't. He is obstinate. And I am too soft. My words are fluid in my mouth, too yielding like the cheese. I have no strength when I tell him that he should ask God for a sign – that the Lord instructs him to ask. But this king only smiles and shakes his head. He says he will not test the Lord. Instead, he is testing me, I am sure of that, but I should not listen to kings. Only to the Lord.

In the dark morning, my ears are alert and I can't stay in bed. I am no good at keeping still. My wife shifts beside me, turns and settles again and I do not want to wake her. The children will be up soon enough. I ease to standing and wrap another layer around my shoulders. When I climb up to the rooftop terrace, I can see the faint beginnings of the day, a hint of lightening grey lying across the sky far away to the east. The city is still hidden, the towers, the palace, the Temple, too, all only smudged shapes or sleeping things against a not-yet-waking sky. Ahaz would be sleeping, too, and let him, I think, pushing him from my mind. Below, the streets must still be dark. Anyone down there would need to walk slowly, feeling their way.

I settle to sit and the rug beneath me is cool and rough. I try to still my mind. I do not begin with prayer, or not with words, at least. I breathe and wait and listen.

I am glad to be alone. There aren't many hours in the day when I can sit unobserved. The students are great observers and I am so rarely left alone. They watch me when I eat, and when I play with my children. They watch me pray, watch me read, watch me listen. Perhaps they are learning something, though some days I wonder. They ask such strange questions. How do I *do* it? Where do I look for words? How do I know what symbols to use? How do I convince my wife to give my sons such names? Yesterday, I found myself talking at length about signs. I said the work was all signs and songs, and they all nodded solemnly and I felt silly. I shouldn't try to sum things up like that. The work isn't like that. It isn't straightforward. I thought then about singing a little, perhaps the new one with the vineyard and the tower. It is a good song and much easier to sing quietly than the ones I sing to Ahaz about idols and ruin and stench. But it did not seem like an afternoon for song so I told them instead how the work comes to me in pieces. Just piece by piece like a child's toy. Like the notched logs my sons play with. You set piece on piece on piece until you see that, without planning, you have built a tower. Things fit together. If you listen, you begin to see how.

A sudden sound, a jump and a scuttle and a cat appears beside me in the greying morning. Seeing him, I know that he wasn't the one who woke me. Something else then. But not a foot in the street, nor the creak of a bucket's handle. The shadow of a song perhaps. Yes, I think so. A strong one. Sitting very still on the cold roof, I begin to see its outlines like the shape of a window in the night, the edge of the morning sky over the city, a door.

The people who walked in darkness have seen a great light;
those who lived in the land of deep darkness –
on them a light has shined.

The song comes slowly, slow as the night passes, but it comes.

Imago Dei

(Genesis 1:27)

It's the best time of the day by far. Halfway home and still a slog ahead of me with the commuter rush to face and then a kid, too, and I don't mind. Not one bit. I wouldn't miss this moment. It's worth everything just to see her face.

Sometimes, I have to look hard to find her in the rush of kids. My curly-headed girl, bright as a button. She's a little one in her class. Her mum says dainty, but I'm sure the kids would all say short. That's fine by me. My sisters were all short and they've managed all right.

To get to the school, I need to sit on the Tube for twenty minutes. I spend that time looking at faces, which isn't something most people do. When I first moved here, I thought everyone looked so sad and so closed. Now I see it's just how you manage in the big city. This city is always moving. It is exhausting, all this crowded travel, all the noise and traffic and worrying about money. And all the eyes that could be looking at you everywhere you go, could be watching. It's easier to look away or not to look at all.

But since she was born, I find myself looking at everything, and wondering, too. Who are all these people? Do they have kids? Where do their parents live? I've become aware of a whole other level of living, just below the surface. Like the Tube, I guess.

The school is a good one, so the playground is always busy. There are lots of clubs and teams for the older kids and it's a bit of a muddle when they come out, before the teachers can gather them together to troop off to wherever it is the clubs take place. I'm sure I'll learn all that when I need to. For the younger kids, it's the parents who make the crowds. Pickup tends to take a while. The teachers are great. Each and every child is individually handed over to the right adult and how the teachers manage to remember all those faces is beyond me. A class of 30 – with parents and grandparents and childminders and whatever else to remember? Amazing.

This time of the year, the playground is cold and grey, but all that changes when the kids come out. Then, it's loud and colourful with candy-cane-sticky grins and hands full of red and green artwork, and all slips of paper with details of parties, fairs and fundraisers. For years, I didn't really notice Christmas. It just wasn't my thing. But now? God, I love it. The unbelievable amount of innocent joy you can cram into one month. Gorgeous. And she gets incandescent with it and I love that, too. Her Christmas concert is next Tuesday, and neither of us can wait. Yesterday, all the way home on the top of the bus, she was singing, but she did it so softly, almost privately, with her head leaning against the bus window. I could see silver glitter in her hair, and smudges of green paint on her fingers as she drew in the fog on the glass, her voice so small and lovely, so secret with delight. She told me not to listen, saying that she wanted all the songs to be a surprise for me. So much love and worth every one of my early mornings.

Now I am looking through the classroom window and I can see the children all sitting together on the rug. Some look tired out, all slumped in their coats. Some are wound up tight, bouncy like springs, ready to be released. Then it happens. You know that moment when they come out through the door and they're flying? Like the cage door has been opened and the birds are all set free. But where is she? All that shifting and moving about and all those uniform school jumpers. Hard to find the little one in all that jumble of kids. And then she turns and I see her. That's my moment. That one, right there. She hasn't seen me yet; she's still looking and only half-listening to the teacher's goodbyes. All the light in my afternoon is in her face.

Do all parents feel this way? They must. Maybe not every day, but everyone must. Isn't it amazing that there is so much love in the world?

So God created humankind in his image, in the image of God he created them; male and female he created them.

Genesis 1:27 (NRSV)

Joe, driving

(Matthew 1:19)

That's all it takes. A map and a plan. Maybe a bumper sticker to keep me smiling. No, Mum, I won't be lonely. I'll be fine. More than fine. This is just something I need to do. Get out of town and see something new. Up north to the hills maybe. I can't think here any more. No, it's not you. Or Dad. I was just fed up, you know? I'm sorry I said all that. I didn't mean it. Yeah, well maybe. Maybe it did have to do with her. I don't know. But I'm okay, though. Really. No, I won't go see her. I wouldn't. I'll give her some space. That's what she wanted, right? So that's what I'll do. I'll drive away, out to where it's wild. But I'll call you. Tonight? Yeah, sure. Just don't call me, though, okay? I need to be alone, and it's not going to feel that way if I know the phone might ring and it might be you. No, I know she's not going to call me. That's not what I'm talking about. I just need to be alone. To drive away and be quiet. Because I don't want to think about what they are saying about her, how they are looking at her now. I don't want to know any of it. Just want an empty road stretching right on ahead of me all flat and level. Like there's going to be a balanced answer. Like nothing's going to fall away.

Her husband Joseph, being a righteous man and unwilling to expose her to public disgrace, planned to dismiss her quietly.

Matthew 1:19 (NRSV)

Step away

Most travel memoirs trace a similar trajectory. Working at a bookshop has taught me that. Someone moves somewhere different. It used to be a man, but nowadays, we read women's stories, too. It is the difference that is important. Different climate, different language, different customs, agricultural, social, culinary, romantic. Or all of the above. The writer discovers the charms and sets out to describe everything and there's lots of space for quaint observation or poetry or recipes. Books like these make you want to move. Well, maybe not everyone. Maybe some people can read these, get a vicarious thrill and leave it at that. And although I don't really have a hankering to go grow olives, or learn how to make pastry in a French woodstove, or put down new roots, well, anywhere really, I still love the idea of flight. Reckless flight.

At this time of year, I like to recommend these books to middle-aged women.

'You've read the one about Italy? Try this one set in northern Spain. There's a great bit in it about the grape harvest in Rioja. You'll love it.'

I imagine her as a woman with a blue overcoat and salt-stained suede boots. I imagine her slipping the purchased book into her briefcase beside the Tupperware now empty of today's office lunch. In the evening, she'll remember the book, and then put the kettle on while her husband loads the dishwasher and he asks her if she knows what's on TV tonight. She doesn't feel like TV tonight. He'll go into the living room, and she'll heat the teapot. She gets out two mugs and the kettle clicks off. She dumps the water from the pot. Two teabags – it's a big pot – and then sugar in his mug because he likes it sweet. She pours his mugful and brings it through to him. He's watching a current affairs programme. When she comes back through to the kitchen, she closes the door, sits down at the table and opens the book. I imagine she enjoys it. Reads slowly. Savours the descriptions. I'm not sure what else. I don't know if she's the type to get really inspired by it. Maybe she does. Maybe she goes off to the library the next day and picks up a pile of cookbooks and makes Spanish meals for the rest of the month. Maybe she plans a trip. It's up to her what happens next. Maybe she just recommends the book to a friend and the author gets a little more in royalties to spend on wine in the local taverna, thanking her lucky stars she had the nerve to step away in the first place.

Loch Sunart – feather

Across the river, leave the main road and into Phemie's Walk. One step at a time until the hills come close. That's how it's done.

We used to walk together. We'd wake up early, pull on our boots and be out walking when the first grey line appeared in the east. I could walk through the trees without worry – hop from stone to stone, even in winter. It is harder now. It will be harder now that she's gone.

Walk under oak. Beech. Larch and fir. Under shadow and ancient growth. Under the arches of fallen trees. Under the weight of days.

There is a sad, old story about this loch that she told me once on a sun-drenched day as we climbed away from the water. A story about a chieftain and a local girl.

'Ah, they are trouble, these local girls,' I said to make her laugh and her eyes were as bright as the day. She told me the chieftain was gallant and brave, and the girl loved him completely, but her mother didn't like the match. Sometimes that's the way with mothers. And maybe this happened so long ago that magic was common, or maybe miracles were thick on the ground that day, but the mother's wishes managed to change her daughter into a swan. Her dress became long white feathers, her fine fingers the spread of wings, and her eyes still dark and shining. The swangirl looked at her mother, but said nothing, only took wing and circled high above the valley, then settled on the water, another white flash among the shining reflections.

When her chieftain love came calling, the girl was nowhere to be seen. *Hunt as you may*, her mother said, *but you will never find her. She has flown.* The chieftain turned away, swearing to return and find his love. He took his bow, his hound and his horn, and he turned towards the hills to spend the day hunting. He chased the red deer and the roe, but all were too swift for him. As the sun dipped behind the hills, he returned to the lake empty-handed and heavy-hearted. Then a flash of white caught his eye. In an instant, his bow was in his hand, the arrow set to flight, for he was sure he'd seen a roe deer. The arrow struck the swangirl and she cried out with her human voice. Only then did he know what his hands had done. She turned and, in turning, appeared again as a girl, her white arms lovely as she sank beneath the waves. He ran into the water, but could not find her, could not pull his love back into life, so he turned his hunting blade on his own pale skin that he, too, might sink and join her under the dark water.

A dark tale, and that's how grief feels.

No swans swim on this loch. Haven't been as long as anyone can remember. That's part of the story, too, I think. You never see them out here. That doesn't make the story true. Nor false. Just a story people like to tell.

So keep climbing, I tell myself, and cross the common grazing land to find the lane running along the rising river. Walk and focus on steps.

The view is lovely, the valley with mist settling on the water and the roofs of houses, the hills and then mountains in the distance. Snow in season, shining white and beautiful in the afternoon light. I don't notice this, but I know it to be true.

I want the steps to work, to make me light again. I want the beauty after grief, the quiet and the time. I want to climb and to be so filled with the sky that I cannot worry about height, about falling.

Somewhere underneath, I want there to be wings.

St Lucy's Day

You come to my door dressed in white, early in the morning. You came last year, too, which makes it a tradition. At your age, a second time does that. *We always, we always,* you say, and your mother catches my eye. We smile.

Your brothers come up behind you with paper lanterns strung on sticks, like luminous fish caught in December's not-quite dawn. They jostle on the step, and I open the door wide to let them in, the morning air outside crisp, clouding our breath, the frost white on the hedge.

Across the street, the milk lorry has pulled up on the pavement, and the man unloads his delivery for the shop. The café around the corner is not yet open. At the end of the street, trees point their bony fingers to the sky.

You linger and smile shyly on the doorstep, the candles on your crown ablaze. They are just electric candles, made of white plastic, and the crown itself is green felt, but you look lovely. You are so excited, standing there with a basket of treats to share, but you are also careful to stand up straight and tall so your crown stays balanced.

This is a new story for me. Lucy and the light. Before I moved here, each December started slowly, bringing memories of my grandmother. Her birthday comes early in the month, and so does the anniversary of her death. Strange how dates can coincide like that. She had forgotten so much by the time she died, so many years collapsed and swept away in confusion. My mum wondered if she might have held on for December, somehow waiting, but not knowing what she waited for.

She would have liked to see you as you are now. She was always kind to small people. You hold out your basket, and I pull back the tea towel to see saffron buns, each twisted like a double snail, the centres marked with currants. There were snails in my granny's garden. I remember that. The broken shells and the thrush's anvil like something out of a fairy tale.

Last year, you told me St Lucy's story – how she visited Christians in the catacombs, wearing a wreath of candles on her head to leave her hands free so that she might carry as much food as possible. Another fairy-tale image, these stories we carry in our hearts.

On the radio this morning, there was a threat of high winds. They might close the bridge, even send the kids home early from school. You'd like that. An afternoon suddenly open for books on the sofa or in your private place behind the curtain. I see you there sometimes when I walk past your house, but don't worry, I won't tell.

Or maybe you will spend the time at the table with your paintbox. This is the season for making cards, of course, and I know you love purple, deep-sky purple, then gold bright like stars. Pop one through my letterbox, will you? I would like to hold it in my hands and look into that light.

> St Lucy was a 3rd-century martyr and her feast day is celebrated on December 13. In Scandinavia, girls dress as St Lucy in long, white gowns and wear wreaths of candles on their heads. They carry baskets of sweet rolls and biscuits to give away as gifts, bringing food and light to neighbours and friends at the beginning of Christmastide.

Jean de Brébeuf

She came with the others at the beginning of the month. Their village had been attacked, they said, and I was not sure if they meant by the Iroquois or the pox. It did not matter. We will always open the gates. They came clutching what they could – a few baskets, cloaks made of skins, small children with wide eyes. She wore a baby tied close to her back, her hair dark and shining, and her face like the moon. She looked calm though her sisters beside her were tired and tense, anxious and unable to be settled even here at the end of their journey. These tall people are proud, but uncertain at our French ways. Or maybe it is our walls that frighten them. Our homes are unlike their long-houses and difference can be difficult. We've had guests before who have travelled days to reach us, looking for rescue, safety and food, only to refuse to enter the gate, preferring to camp out in the cornfields. It was only through much prayer and much patience that they joined us behind the wooden fence, to share the food from our kitchens and the warmth of our fires.

The pox has been cruel throughout this summer. So many Wendat villages have suffered and many people have come to us seeking help. They call me Echon, which means *healing tree,* and this name has spread as has news of our home here with its strong walls. Many have come expecting miracles. But I cannot make the pox go away, as they assert, or bring the rain. I would prefer to think that they gave me the name simply because I am tall and not because they expect me to work magic. I only hold hands and pray. I sit close and find courage. I pray for better strength.

Later, I saw her sitting on her own with the child. He was wrapped in skins and lay in her arms and she bent her face toward him, her smooth cheek on his new skin, her eyes closed and adoring. The moon, I thought again, or the Virgin. Is such a thought sin? I should perhaps confess it to one of the others. They are used to hearing my sins. Sins of omission, mainly. I spend too much time listening to these people, hearing their stories and learning the shape of their words. I spend too little time preaching and our numbers of baptism are very low. We were sent here to New France to spread the faith and I focus too much on learning languages and hearing the stories of other peoples. These are my habitual confessions. Perhaps I should add to this the sin of imagining the Virgin in a native girl's face. But no. There is no desolation here and there can be no more sin to see Her here in the face of a young mother than in a piece of glass in a Rouen church. She wills that we think of Her and pray with Her everywhere, and She is forever showing us Her face. She is the Beautiful Translator, is She not? Cradling the Living Word in all times and in all places.

> Jean de Brébeuf (1593-1649) was a Jesuit missionary to the Wendat people in what is now southern Ontario, Canada. He wrote the first Canadian Christmas Carol, 'Iesus Ahatonnia', which is a retelling of the Nativity story from an indigenous perspective and in the Wendat language:
>
> *'The star stopped not far from where Jesus was born.*
> *Having found the place, it said,*
> *"Come this way."*
> *Jesus, he is born.*
>
> *As they entered and saw Jesus they praised his name.*
> *They oiled his scalp many times, anointing his head*
> *with the oil of the sunflower.*
> *Jesus, he is born.'*
>
> Reworked into English by Jesse Edgar Middleton in 1926, the hymn is now known as 'The Huron Carol'.

Elisabeth watches the hoopoes

(Luke 1:57–58)

They should have left long ago, but they are still here. I check every morning, though the light is weak in the courtyard, my fingers stiff and the cold latch awkward. And every morning, they are there, sitting up on the branch, their feathered crests like crowns bright in the wintering daylight. I wonder if they always stay and if I haven't noticed. Last winter, I stayed inside, barely wanting to move in case, well, just in case. I felt too old for all that growth, unready, unsteady and Zechariah was silent, so I suppose I also felt alone. The birds might have helped, had I noticed them.

My mother loved these birds, and she would never listen when my father said they were unlucky. 'King Solomon's favourites,' she'd crow. 'Confidants of the king and that shows wisdom.' But these ones in the garden can't be wise, lingering long into the winter like this. The mornings are cold now, and it takes until the afternoon for the sun to come into the courtyard.

But then, I take the boy outside to play under the tree, sitting him up on the warmed stones where we can watch the birds. They have their nest in a hole in the wall and they come and go over our heads. There are two of them, and I'm never sure which I am seeing; they are so similar. Their call makes the boy laugh. *Hoo-hoo-poe, hoo-hoo-poo.* Then their wings are a wheel of black and white, and he beams like he's seeing angels and claps his hands. He is growing so quickly now. Already pulling himself up to his feet, pushing the chair across the room. They say that boys are slow to walk, but not my boy. I shouldn't speak that aloud. It isn't fair to compare. But he is bright and we are blessed.

My thoughts are with my cousin now. She must be coming close. I wanted to be there for her, but Zechariah said it was proper to leave them be. The girl was with us long enough, he said, and there was enough talk. He doesn't understand. Yet perhaps it is all for the best. They've had to travel for this census, and, in the end, I wouldn't have been able to travel with them.

I hope she has others around her when it is her time. I had my helpers, and the midwife, too, a girl with strong arms to hold me as I quaked into that long night. She rubbed my back and helped me to sing, a low and calling melody so that he would know that the world was ready to make space for him, too. I wonder who will sing with Mary.

My mother taught me that the hoopoes are loved in Egypt, even if the priests here don't fancy them. She said they lay twelve eggs each year, small, round and blue like scraps of the sky itself, smuggled down and nurtured until the chicks can push into tender life, grow thick with feathers and fly away. I think she loved them because they are beautiful. Maybe that is enough.

Now the time came for Elisabeth to give birth, and she bore a son. Her neighbours and relatives heard that the Lord had shown his great mercy to her, and they rejoiced with her.

Luke 1:57–58 (NRSV)

Death crowns

You can't tell from the weight of the pillow. You have to rip it open.

When you hold it in your hands, you just wonder like you might wonder about ripening fruit. Then you pull the seams, pull until it tears and you let the feathers fly and hope and hope that you might find a crown.

I read about this ritual in a magazine on the train. Didn't think I could concentrate on anything long, anything complicated, not that day, so I'd picked up a magazine at the station. Travel-themed with pretty photos and weird stories. I like that kind of thing. I found my seat, a window one which felt lucky, kept my coat on, and spent the time flipping pages.

A photograph of the feather wreath caught me. It was a twisted thing, a crafted loop of interlacing quills and, set against a sky-blue background, it looked like a halo.

Death crowns, they call them. They appear in the pillows of the dead, it seems. They are lucky. Messages from angels. Signs of hope. When the room is aired and the bedding removed, the pillow is lifted and torn open. If a crown is found, the mourners know that heaven has come close.

You only find them in the Appalachians in the American South, though the magazine writer mentioned the tradition might have its roots in Welsh folklore. Mostly, you see them in museums and sometimes they turn up in junk shops tucked away in careful boxes, saved and reassuring. They aren't found so much these days. I guess there just aren't so many feather pillows.

I looked out the train window. Dark birds in a ploughed field. A flash of bright water and geese flying. In the distance, a hill.

Maybe it's only the tossing of a fevered head, I thought. That might form a feathered ring. Just a final restlessness with death's own ringing step echoing on the stair.

The magazine photo showed a landscape green with mountains, and thick with trees. There must be valleys hidden between the hills; lakes and rivers, too, and people, but all you could see in the photo was layers and layers of green mountains.

My weekend case sat in the luggage rack and I hoped my dress didn't wrinkle too much. Mum could lend me an iron in the morning if I needed it.

In an hour, I'd be home. The rest of the family would be there already. For dinner we'd order pizza, hold hands, plan speeches, and wonder. The next day there'd be stories and whisky, but that first night together we'd all be tired.

The train kept heading east with me thinking and thinking about those southern hills and their hidden valleys, the mornings blue as smoke. I wondered if there were wild geese down there and if the creeks froze up in the winter.

Later, when the visit was almost over and it was time to go back home, I stood in the doorway, looking into the back room of my grandparents' house. I could see my grandfather's chair, still sitting by the bookcase. Its worn back was caved with the weight of his head, the seat slack, the arms rough with shifted horsehair stuffing. My grandmother stood by the window, scissors in her hand. She'd been deadheading the geraniums on the sill. Their flowers were crumpled spiders now, dung-brown and dry, snipped, collected and hidden away in the pocket of her apron.

She said you need to let them go. The blooms don't last, though the leaves do, all winter long, soft and green, shedding their tomato fragrance in the closed room.

I stood in that doorway listening, still in my good shoes, the last of the visitors leaving, looking into all these unknown countries.

He never comes for Christmas

He never comes for Christmas. Not even when I tell him that we could really use the help. Not on your life. Wouldn't darken the door, he says. The girls are a handful now and Danny and I are stretched pretty thin. But no. Not even for the grandkids. Won't budge. Churches are for the simple-minded and he won't condone that kind of nonsense. Then he says it would be easier to stay home anyway, wouldn't it, and he raises a sceptical eyebrow, giving me that old, familiar look. Indulgent. It drives me crazy and I hate it, but I love him. I love him. There it is. My bonkers atheist dad with his zest for the good life.

I won't change him. Wouldn't hope to try. But couldn't he tag along to church once in a while? For me?

At Christmas, I wonder if Easter might be easier. Not Good Friday or anything solemn. Just Easter Sunday itself when the church is beautiful with lilies and light and the air is warm and fragrant. When you can practically breathe in resurrection and believe it with every atom. But no. He'd rather be in France. He'll come visit later. Maybe in June. He'll take us to the seaside then and it will be ice creams and donkey rides all round.

So I sit in the pew at Easter, gripping the wriggling kids in their seersucker dresses and think ahead to Christmas. Maybe it will be better then. Maybe I can convince him that we'd rather have him with us than a heap of gifts under the tree. Just come along, that's all I want. I could argue it would be cheaper. I could tell him that mum would have liked it. I could tell a thousand stories, but nothing's going to change. Not when it comes to my dad.

Danny said maybe it's like seeing colour. Some folk can't. No one chooses to be colour-blind and maybe it's the same way for faith. Danny's good at standing up for my dad, which is a good trait in a husband, I guess. Keeps me warm.

Adam, naming

(Genesis 2:19)

I'll tell you how it feels. Like a bulb tucked away in the soil. Like a hand in a pocket or salt in bread. Like a bucket returned to the well. It feels right.

Whenever I find the right name for a bird, a new wild flower, a shape in the clouds, it feels right and fitting. This has always been my work and I guess it always will be. In the beginning, it felt like singing. Names came in quick succession, note on note on note, tumbling and racing, making me laugh with their energy as they flew out into the world and settled in each place, on each face, perfectly. I laughed and God was smiling and all was well. Spring and summer, growth and fruitfulness, then harvest, too, with all good names.

After the garden and the green, names grew harder, but the work was still left in my hands. The soil was heavy and my fingernails caked in dirt as I learned to dig. The skin of my face cracked in the wind, and the weather was unkind, and still all these things needed names. Earth and wind and weather with all its faces. I worry their names like beads in my hand. It is good work. It's always been good work and now I wonder about the end, because we've been told there will be one. You will finish the planting, and pruning for the winter, and I will leave aside the plough. Our turn will be over and the boys will begin theirs. And the names? Will the boys continue this work, too? I suppose they will.

But you asked me how it feels and I have given you some of an answer, but not all. The struggle is hard. Like heaving stones out of a field, their rough surfaces against my skin, my back braced against their weight. Or like shearing sheep. I trim away the softness until something clear and clean jumps forth, suddenly evident, and more often than not, scrambling away until it is only a smudge of white against a faraway hillside. It feels like these winter days and the struggle through the snow to make sure the ewes have hay, and find a wall where they can shelter or a tree with low, sweeping branches that can hold back the wind. It feels like my worry for their unborn lambs, growing heavier each day as their mothers grow weary with winter. It feels slow and surprising and something like love.

And you. I called you Eve, my love and my dear one. I called you the mother of life. Life flows through you, and you are lovely. You grow fat with life, full as the beautiful moon and just as bright. But now I am afraid of death. Shadowed, dusty, breaking death. The end that comes because we wait or the end that comes more quickly. You are the fragrance of new leaves and fresh hills and smoke, salt and sweetness and bread. I watch you with the boys, holding each one in turn, breathing them in, these running, tumbling boys of ours, so full of your life. I've seen the look in your eyes. I understand. But we will need to let go. They will grow older, too. Take wives, bear children. In turn, they will hold them each close against their own hearts and breathe in the fragrance of sweat and wool and storms and honey. And their children, too, will be held and their children and theirs in coming days, as all of time unfolds.

So out of the ground the Lord God formed every animal of the field and every bird of the air; and he brought them to the man to see what he would call them; and whatever the man called every living creature, that was its name.

Genesis 2:19 (NRSV)

Simeon and Anna

(Luke 2:22)

He's a lovely man, a right man of God. Righteous and devout. No one knows how old he is, just that he has always been here in Jerusalem. As old as the hills, he says with a twinkle. Or as old as his tongue and a little older than his teeth. He knows how to make us laugh.

He is patient, too, which helps when it gets crowded around here. The pilgrims get anxious and want to know they are in the right place, that they are paying the right price for the right sacrifice, and that their prayers will be heard. He always has a kind word for them. Says the Lord loves them, even if they fill the place with noise, worry and hesitations. He doesn't mind the pigeons or the flies, does He? Then why should these people be a bother? Let them fuss and we'll focus on what matters, shall we?

Simeon says we have all the time in the world.

He likes to use a poetic turn of phrase, which makes him a bit old-fashioned. They say he has always been like that, playing with language the way weavers tease wool back and forth, and patterns emerge. Some even say that he was among the seventy who translated the Law and the Prophets into Greek. Maybe, maybe, though it is hard to fathom anyone could be so ancient. He certainly knows the texts well enough and that's useful in these difficult empire days. We are not an easy people, and this is not an easy city. There's a hunger about Jerusalem. The exile is ended, of course, and the city has been rebuilt for years, but things aren't yet right. Rome's hand is heavy and God's word is quiet. There are so many distractions for the people these days, and so many temptations. People do still aim to be faithful, though perhaps fewer than before, and though the Temple is still a busy place, we struggle with politics. Maybe it has ever been thus. I am glad that, in these days, there is a man like Simeon on whom the Spirit rests.

We see each other most days, sometimes in the marketplace but usually at the Temple. Since my husband died, I have spent much of my time here. It is a good place to pray and prayer is a good way to spend the days. Simeon says it is at prayer that we learn to listen. When he first said that to me, I didn't understand. I was working on remembering all the words and getting them in the right order. Listening didn't seem to be part of it. But then I learned. The words are only there to get the heart in order. They neaten things up, make straight lines and channels. A bit like gardening or farming, I suppose. And then your heart is ready when the Lord comes. He comes like rain, like rivers of water, rushing through, bringing life. Even to an old widow like me, He comes. That's what Jerusalem needs. It's what the world needs, isn't it? A right good downpour because we're all so thirsty. Simeon says he's been hearing rumours – and I told him not to be a foolish old man and that maybe he'd better stay away from the marketplace – but he told me they were rumours of God. He heard them first in his work with the Law and the Prophets – peppered with rumours, he said, rumours of something new, something wonderful coming soon. Consolation. And he tells me that the rumours aren't just written; they are also heard in the heart. He heard a promise – like an angel whispering over his shoulder as he worked on the Law – that he would not die until he had seen salvation with his own eyes. He remembers the day clearly, and the text, too. The prophet wrote 'Behold, a virgin shall conceive ...' and he hesitated, hearing something, something all those years ago.

But where was I? Simeon is a good man. Yes, that was it. He waits and he listens and he believes, even in these troubled times. I must tell the priests all this, because they are worried. Too often, they say, he is found asleep in the courtyard, propped up against a pillar, his mouth agape. I am sure they worry that he will die there and then the Temple will need to be cleansed. There must be laws against dying in the Temple. All old men, scribes or prophets, must withdraw and find a dignified place to breathe their last. Ah well, I will tell them. Perhaps this afternoon.

Simeon is awake now, and I watch him approach a young couple, coming to make an offering by the looks of it. The husband carries the doves and the wife holds their baby close, looking around with wide eyes at the height and splendour of the Temple. It looks as if she is watching for something, as if she expects something miraculous to happen. Simeon smiles warmly, ready as always to show them which way to go.

Salvation will be like this, I think. Like the mystery of welcome and the new-ness of a child. Because a newborn child is real and yet not real. You can't take your eyes off him but you can't see who he will be. Might even say here and not yet here. But we will hold out our arms to welcome the new, and in that shining moment, I think we will know God.

When the time came for their purification according to the law of Moses, they brought him up to Jerusalem to present him to the Lord ...

Luke 2:22 (NRSV)

In many churches, the Presentation of Jesus at the Temple is cele-brated as Candlemas on February 2. In the Eastern Orthodox Church,

Simeon and Anna are commemorated on February 3 on the Feast of the Holy and Righteous, Simeon the God-Receiver and Anna the Prophetess.

And so we begin

We're all straining our eyes for a new way to start. That's how people are. Living out our days in blocks of time, waiting for the future to begin. This month and then … To the end of this season and … It will be different then and I will be different and things will be new. Again and again and again.

This move has been a good new beginning for me. Sudden, and maybe that's best when it comes to newness. When the opportunity at the college opened up, something inside me opened up, too, and I jumped. Then only two weeks to get everything packed and planned and all my goodbyes said. No time for doubts and regrets amidst a hundred little details and I only just managed to sit down on Sunday morning, one last Sunday at church after all our years together.

Lord, you have been our dwelling place in all generations. Those were the words that caught my attention that morning. They sounded old as the hills and fresh as the morning in a single folded moment. God as our dwelling place. I like that. So, I've been carrying those words around ever since, tumbling them around in my brain and seeing how they sit. They come from Psalm 90, but the preacher said they were the words of Moses and that's what it says in my Bible, too. And maybe that's why I held them. Like me,

Moses was a travelling man. A man of faith, too, as I try to be. He must have known a thing or two about moving on and the search for beginnings.

This city is a good place for beginnings. So many new kinds of people, every shade and shape, speaking so many new languages. New for me, that is. I could spend a year walking these streets just listening. And the food! So many new flavours and new fragrances. They follow me around, trip me up, track me down, slip into the folds of my clothes, my hair, my hands, sweet, sticky, strong, salty. So much to eat. So wonderful.

But I promised myself I would tell you a story. Just a snapshot, a postcard from this new city and this new life of mine.

This happened on my first evening here. I had the keys to my flat and was hungry, of course, so I went out to find something to eat. Not a restaurant meal or a bag of groceries. I went looking for street food like we'd find at home. Everywhere I turned, every corner, every street, there were so many lights. I walked and walked and couldn't stop looking. I even forgot I was hungry, that's how new the city felt. Snow had fallen late in the afternoon and now the streetlights made it shine. Every tree branch, every horizontal surface was traced in pure white.

On the corner, there was a bookshop. The sign on the door said *Closed*, and inside, I could see a bucket with a mop propped up against the glass. The lights were all on in the shop, and a man with a face like mine stood with a book in his hands and leaned back against a shelf. His ankles were crossed and his glasses sat perched low on his nose. He looked up and saw me through the window, his face motionless, his finger on the page. For a long moment, we stood there watching each other like visitors at a late-night aquarium or kids at the cookie jar. Then, an ambulance drove through the intersection behind me, tearing open the night with red lights and noise. We both turned to watch, and when it was gone, I turned back to the street and walked away.

Every evening since then, I have thought about that man and wondered where he was from and what he was reading.

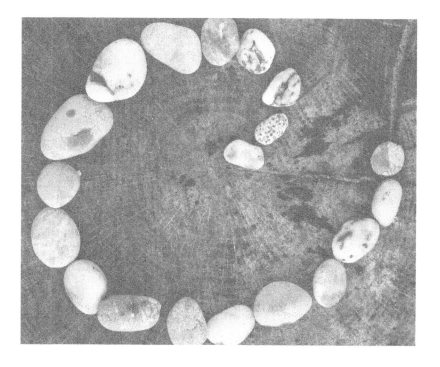

Acknowledgements

Versions of the following pieces have appeared previously in these publications: 'Grey' in *Amaryllis*; 'Sacred heart' in *Geez Magazine*; 'Melangell's lambs' in *Glad Tidings*; 'A letter to the person under the train', 'Wasp', 'Might', and 'Isaiah, listening' in *The Presbyterian Record*; 'St Lucy's Day' and 'Elisabeth watches the hoopoes' in *Winter* (Wild Goose Publications). 'Swimming' was featured by Seren Books as Short Story of the Month in July 2017. 'Mary's Palm Sunday' was written and performed as part of *Palm Sunday Stooshie*, a travelling play with the Spark Festival in Edinburgh, March 2015. Characters and segments of other stories have been shared in various communities and congregations in the UK and Canada, including Canongate Kirk, Nitekirk and the Scottish Storytelling Centre in Edinburgh; St Columba's Church, London; St Andrew's Presbyterian Church and Knox Presbyterian Church, Ottawa.

Wild Goose Publications, the publishing house of the Iona Community established in the Celtic Christian tradition of Saint Columba, produces books, e-books, CDs and digital downloads on:

- holistic spirituality
- social justice
- political and peace issues
- healing
- innovative approaches to worship
- song in worship, including the work of the Wild Goose Resource Group
- material for meditation and reflection

For more information:

Wild Goose Publications
The Iona Community
21 Carlton Court, Glasgow, G5 9JP, UK

Tel. +44 (0)141 429 7281
e-mail: admin@ionabooks.com

or visit our website at
www.ionabooks.com
for details of all our products and online sales